General Editor:
Patrick McNeill

Age and Generation

Mike O'Donnell

* Statistics
* Comparison features.
* Views of teenagers
* Teenage life

APROVEL®

AGE AND
GENERATION

Tavistock Publications · *London* · *New York*

19350
021272

To Dylan: From His Old Man

First published in 1985 by
Tavistock Publications Ltd
11 New Fetter Lane,
London EC4P 4EE

Published in the USA by
Tavistock Publications
in association with Methuen, Inc.
733 Third Avenue,
New York, NY 10017

© 1985 Mike O'Donnell

Typeset in Great Britain by
Activity Limited, Salisbury, Wilts
and printed by
Richard Clay, The Chaucer Press,
Bungay, Suffolk

*British Library Cataloguing in
Publication Data*

O'Donnell, Mike
Age and generation. – (Society now) –
(Social science paperbacks; no. 301)
1. Age groups – Social aspects
I. Title II. Series III. Series
305.2 GN490.5

ISBN 0–422–79360–4

Contents

Acknowledgements

The author and publishers would like to thank the following for permission to reproduce copyright material: Routledge & Kegan Paul and Harcourt Brace Jovanovich, New York for Table 1 reproduced from B. Malinowski *The Sexual Life of Savages*, 1957; Weidenfeld and Nicolson for Figure 1 reproduced from P. Abrams *Work, Urbanism, and Inequality: UK Society Today*, 1978, adapted from B. S. Rowntree *Poverty: A Study of Town Life* Macmillan, 1901; Harcourt Brace Jovanovich, Florida for Table 2 reproduced from S. R. Hilgard *Introduction to Psychology*, 1979, adapted from Erikson *Childhood and Society*, 2nd edn 1963, W. W. Norton, New York; Commission of the European Communities for Table 4 reproduced from *The Young Europeans*, 1982; the Commission for Racial Equality for Tables 5 and 7 adapted from *Race Relations in 1981*, 1981; HMSO for Table 6 reproduced from *The Rampton Report*, 1981, *Cmnd 8273*.

Preface

I would like to thank Caroline Riddell, Sandra den Hertog, and Joy Outten for typing the final manuscript of this book. They achieved deadlines with greater ease and patience than the author.

I have had this book – or something like it – in my mind for some years but I am grateful to the series editor, Patrick McNeill, for prompting me to write it. He also provided the necessary second pair of eyes to help me assess my work as it was being produced. Patricia Mayes, too, commented helpfully on the early chapters.

My students responded constructively to much of the following material. However, I need to acknowledge their influence on more than one account. I have written the sections on youth with an acute awareness of the difficulties and challenges facing them and their contemporaries.

Economic and educational policy and developments have changed the position of young people radically. A major aim of this book is to help them link these changes to their own situations and experiences. Only connect!

Mike O'Donnell

1

Age and generation

Few would disagree with S.N. Eisenstadt's comment that 'Age and differences of age are among the most basic and crucial aspects of human life and determinants of human destiny' (Eisenstadt 1956). In everyday life we are, perhaps, as conscious of age differences as we are of those of class or gender. The latter we may take for granted, but ageing is a continuous process the consequences of which keep confronting us. Despite its obvious importance, age has not been explored by sociologists as thoroughly as might be expected.

The sociology of age is about the experience and treatment of age groups in society. The concept of *age group* is the broadest term used to refer to an aggregate of people differentiated from others according to age. Sociologists accept the biological reality of age and concentrate on how it is socially structured. As we shall see, age groups – children, the young, the old – are treated differently in different societies. The comparative aspect of the sociology of age is essential in establishing the role of culture in age stratification. For instance, comparative analysis shows that it is not biologically inevitable that the old should have little power and prestige, as they do in many areas of western societies. Why this is so is an interesting sociological question.

Despite their primary interest in the social sphere, sociologists generally recognize that age groups are a product of the *interaction* of biological and social factors. Karl Mannheim's remark on the concept of generation applies to age in general: 'The sociological phenomenon of generations is ultimately based on the biological rhythm of birth and death' (Mannheim 1952). Biology sets certain general limits to behaviour. Thus leading warriors or athletes are seldom, if ever, recruited from the very old or the very young in any society. I will present Mannheim's own model of the relationship between biology and age shortly.

A generation is a form of age group. Tavistock's *A Dictionary of the Social Sciences* provides us with a definition of the broadest usage of the term: 'A generation comprises all those members of a society who were born approximately at the same time, whether or not they are related by blood.' Generation is also used to refer to the period between those born at the same time and the birth of their children, usually assumed by social scientists to be about thirty years.

Mannheim (1893–1947) distinguishes between generation as *location* and generation as *actuality*. The former means the same as the broadest usage of the term – to coexist or be located with others of the same age. A generation as an actuality shares a community of experience and feeling. Mannheim published his analysis of generation in the 1920s, but it is possible to give a modern example of what he means. The almost universal emotional involvement of American youth in the Vietnam War provides a modern example of an *actual* generational experience. Mannheim points out that such experiences tend to occur at a very general level. He introduced the concept of *generation unit* to provide more

2

specific analysis. Generational units share an identity of responses and views about events. Thus there were various pro- and anti-war units within the 'Vietnam War generation'. Mannheim (1952) puts the difference between a generational unit and an actual generation as follows:

> 'The generation unit represents a much more concrete bond than the actual generation as such. Youth experiencing the same concrete historical problems may be said to be part of the same actual generation, while those groups within the same actual generation which work up the material of their common experience in different specific ways constitute separate generation units.'

Age groups in simple societies

The purpose of this section is to illustrate some of the differences and similarities in age groupings in simple and modern societies. It is not a representative overview of age in simple societies.

The age-grade system which occurs in *some* simple societies provides a contrast with the less formal structuring of age common in modern societies, yet in Eisenstadt's view it fulfils the same function – to maintain social solidarity. According to A.R. Radcliffe-Brown (1952), an age grade is 'the recognized division of the life of the individual as he passes from infancy to old age'. Thus male aborigines pass through the age grades of hunter, warrior, and elder. Each of these age divisions or grades involves certain duties and rights, and a degree of prestige in relation to other grades. The exact age span and activities of age grades vary between societies, but wherever they occur there is a point at which the young person acquires full adult status. This occasion is always marked by an initiation ritual or rite of passage, although these rites also occur in certain non-age-grade simple societies. An age set denotes the group of persons initiated during the same period within a given age-grade system. The age set advances together through the age-grade system. Ceremonies relating to major transitions in life, such as birth, the coming of age, marriage, and death, are of central and sacred significance in simple societies.

It is worth quoting part of Kenneth Maddock's account of the Bora, or male initiation ceremony, of the Murring, an aboriginal tribe:

'The Murring Bora was theatrically among the most brilliant of the Australian initiatory cults .... Howitt (1883), who described the Murring version, used Bora as a generic name for man-making cults in south-east Australia. Their central rite was physically to mark the candidate by removing a tooth, but they enclosed this act in a series of rites dramatizing the shift in his life away from women and children and towards men. These cults are extinct, but their procedures and processes have much in common with what happens in the living initiation ritual of other parts of Australia ....

Teeth were removed at a spot out of sight from the fire. The novices were taken to where a row of pairs of holes had been dug and each was made to stand in a pair while his guardian stood close behind him. A line of men knelt before the novices, the man at each end holding a strip of bark with which he could produce a report like a firearm by striking a heap of earth in front of him. These men wore sheets of yellow fibre from the stringybark. Only their faces remained visible, and they were distorted by strings tied across the nose and lips. On a large tree to one side of this place could be seen the dancing figure of Daramulun, the All-Father, cut into the bark.

The scene thus set, the presiding elder signalled to the man at one end of the kneeling line to crack his strip of bark. The others surged away from him, rumbling in imitation of the roar of surf. The man at the other end cracked his strip of bark and they surged back, imitating this time the roll of

4

thunder. After this had continued for some time the men leapt to their feet and rushed to the novices. Each was made to sit on his guardian's knee while another gripped him from behind with the right arm and blindfolded him with the left. To the accompaniment of excited dancing an operator emerged from hiding and danced forward with the wooden "mallet" and "chisel" used for removing teeth. From each novice he tapped out an upper incisor, loosening it first by inserting beneath it his own lower incisors and wrenching upwards. After the novices all had suffered this ordeal they were led to the dancing figure of the All-Father to be instructed about him.'   (Maddock 1973: 137, 139)

The removal of a tooth, which might seem a needless injury to westerners, is a powerful symbol to the Murring: it is the visible imprint of manhood. Referring to such ceremonies, Malinowski (1957) writes of tribal authority being 'hammered into the body'. Other aboriginal tribes adopt distinctive markings, such as circumcision or scarification. However, the visible marking does not complete the transition to adulthood. Invisible 'markings', consisting of the instruction and reformation of the mind and character, are also prescribed. Both visible and invisible markings are necessary before a man can represent in ritual the powers of his clan.

In contrast, there is no rite of passage to adulthood in modern societies like Britain and the United States. There is not even a specific legal age when a young person becomes an adult. Nevertheless, as we shall see, the stage of youth in modern societies is no less important. (I prefer to use the term age group rather than age grade (or age class) to describe age stages in modern society because, despite their importance, they are less formally structured than age grades in simple societies.)

Eisenstadt argues that it is the function of age grades and other strong forms of age groups (as in modern societies) to contribute to the stability and harmony of society (Eisenstadt 1956). They develop in those societies where there is a difference between kinship values of particularism, ascription, and role diffuseness, and work values of universalism, achievement, and role specificity. This break occurs in some simple societies and virtually all modern ones. Thus age grades and strong age groupings provide a buffer zone. They give support and identity but are also orientated towards adult work roles. In contrast, kinship societies are simple societies in which work is organized by the family-kinship system and they rarely develop age grades (though see below). The wide-spreading kinship system provides the necessary social solidarity, though within it age is usually an important factor in determining position and seniority.

Eisenstadt presents two 'hypotheses' which suggest the types of society in which age groups are likely to occur. His first is that 'Age groups tend to arise in those societies whose main integrative principles are different from the particularistic principles governing family and kinship relations, i.e. in societies whose integrative principles are mainly "universalistic".' In other words, age groups occur in societies in which economic and, usually, political life are organized (integrated) on the basis of general rules (universalism) rather than the personal (particularistic) values of the family-kinship system. Thus in modern society, jobs are allocated on the basis of qualifications and experience (achievement) rather than title of birth (ascription). Modern capitalist societies, for instance, function on the basis of universalistic principles (some embodied in law) governing individual competition. Importantly, youth provides a transitional zone between the very different 'worlds' of the family-kinship system and the economic system.

The second instance in which Eisenstadt argues that age groups tend to arise need not detain us long as it applies only to familistic societies (societies in which nearly all roles are organized within the kinship system). In his words: 'Age groups tend to arise when the structure of the family or descent groups blocks the younger members' opportunities for attaining social status within the family.' The age group then becomes an alternative source of status and a basis for organizing generational conflict.

To return to Eisenstadt's first instance of age groups: its most relevant application for us is to modern society which is 'the fullest example of a universalistically regulated society'. It is important to note, however, that universalistic tendencies can occur in simple and traditional societies, and Eisenstadt gives many examples of strongly structured age groups (in some cases formal age-grade systems) arising in such societies. Frankly, this point is often obscured in textbook presentations of Eisenstadt's work. His main contrast is between the structuring of age in universalistic (including some non-modern) and particularistic societies, not between exclusively modern and pre-modern societies.

Age groups in universalistically inclined societies contribute to social stability and harmony. Thus youth provides a context in which both personal and diffuse (not tied to a specific role) behaviour, similar to that in the family, and more specific role preparation (e.g. for work) are permitted. As Einstadt puts it, age groups provide 'primary solidarity groups .... which are partly defence against future roles and partly oriented towards them .... Their function is to extend the solidarity of the kinship system to the whole social system through emphasis on diffuse age-group membership.'

We must now review Eisenstadt's classic contribution to the sociology of generation. First, it needs to be assessed as a piece of positivist sociology which attempts to test two hypotheses about why age groups arise in certain societies. I am not aware that a full critique of this kind has yet been made – possibly because of the huge scope and detail of his work – so judgement must be reserved on this point. Second, Eisenstadt's analysis of the youthful age group as contributing to social solidarity has been widely influential. However, he is inadequate when dealing with conflict between youth groups and social control agencies. In this matter, class-based analyses seem more illuminating (see Chapter 3). Third, the notion of modern youth as a stage of transition perhaps appeared almost self-evidently true in the mid-1950s, when Eisenstadt's work was published. It seems less so now when massive youth unemployment provokes the question 'transition to what?' We cannot draw out of Eisenstadt an explanation of the roles of contemporary youth or the functions of their unemployment.

Eisenstadt's main hypothesis suggests that sharply differentiated age grades or classes do not usually develop in kinship societies. Although only one case, Bronislaw Malinowski's study of Trobriand Island society, supports Eisenstadt: it was a kinship society characterized by neither clearly defined age grades nor initiation ceremonies. Malinowski observed broad age designations which, as an examination of *Table 1* should indicate, are similar to those recognizable in modern societies. However, if the general age categories designated by Malinowski are familiar, the roles associated with them are often strikingly different from western patterns. I shall illustrate this when I discuss specific stages in the life-cycle.

Stages in the life-cycle

The concept of the life-cycle is a biological one. Our use of it shows again that the study of age is interdisciplinary in nature. The life-cycle indicates the progression and rough phasing of biological and psychological developments in the individual. However, no individual lives outside society; therefore study of the life-cycle is of the interaction of physical, psychological, and social phenomena. Our specific interest here is in how society structures particular stages in the life-cycle or, in other words, the social construction of age.

There is no universal consensus on what precise stages the life-cycle should be divided into, although there is some measure of agreement among both expert and common-sense opinion. How people divide the age span varies to some extent with age itself, as do views of what is young and old. Thus, children often make do with three categories: childhood, adulthood, and old age. Adults, however, will nearly always distinguish between adulthood and adolescence, and differen-

Table 1   *Designations of age*

		I stage: *Gwadi* – word used as a generic designation for all these stages 1–4, meaning *child*, male or female, at any time between birth and maturity
1	*Wayuvaya* (foetus; infant till the age of crawling, both male and female)	
2	*Pwapwawa* (infant, till the stage of walking, male or female)	
3	*Gwadi* (child, till puberty, male or female)	
4	*Inaguvadi* (female child)	
	Monaguvadi (male child)	
5	*Nakapugula* or *Nakubuk-wabuya* (girl from puberty till marriage)	II stage: generic designations – *Ta'u* (man), *Vivila* (woman)
5	*To'ulatile* (youth from puberty till marriage)	
6	*Nabubowa'u* (ripe woman)	
6a	*Navavaygile* (married woman)	
6	*Tobubowa'u* (mature man)	
6a	*Tovavaygile* (married man)	
7	*Numwaya* (old woman)	III stage: old age
7	*Tomwaya* (old man)	
7a	*Toboma* (old honoured man)	

Source: Malinowski (1957: 51).

tiate early and middle adulthood. Age and age categories are perceived differently in different cultures, and differently in the same society over time. Illustrating the relative nature of cultural perceptions of age, Philippe Ariès writes: 'In the African bush, age is still quite an obscure notion, something that is not so important that one cannot forget it' (Ariès 1962). On the point of changing perceptions of age, Ariès argues that the 'idea of childhood' is substantially a modern phenomenon and particularly a twentieth-century one. The same argument has frequently been made about the creation of 'youth as a stage of life' (see pp. 25–6).

We must, therefore, treat cautiously any division of the life-cycle into stages. It may be that the progression of certain physical and even psychological developments is universal to our species, but the social significance given to these stages varies greatly. Indeed, as Ariès implies, the recognition of a particular age span as a 'stage' depends on social perception. Nevertheless, Erik Erickson's characterization of development as a series of eight stages is generally regarded as a useful and well-informed presentation of the life-cycle in modern societies. Erickson himself believes it has wider application still. I will use the model as a general framework for analysing various stages in the life-cycle.

The social structuring of stages in the life-cycle is the central topic of this book. Before analysing specific stages, it will help to consider how, in capitalist societies, the life-cycle as a whole is structured by the way work is organized relative to age. Over eighty years ago, Seebohm Rowntree showed that the incidence of poverty was a function of the relationship between the labour market and the life-cycle. Thus the low paid dropped below the poverty line during certain phases in the life-cycle, such as that following the birth of children and after retirement (see *Figure 1*). Broadly, the same relationship persists today.

As Philip Abrams points out, not much can be done to change the life-cycle, but social and economic policy can affect low pay and the poverty that afflicts large numbers of old people. Society can do much to ensure that people of a certain

Figure 1   Poverty and the life-cycle

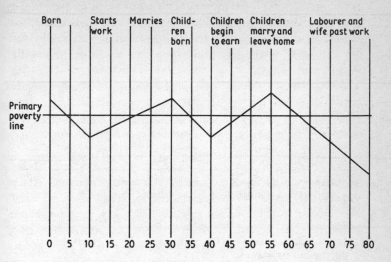

Source: adapted from Rowntree (1901) in Abrams (1978:9).

age in given circumstances do not suffer poverty – by changing the circumstances.

Further reading

Philip Abrams has published two clear general essays on age: first, 'Age and Generation' in Barker (1972), and second, pp. 5–10 in his 'Introduction' to Abrams (1978). See also O'Donnell (1981), Chapter 13, 'Generation', which gives a basic introduction to the topic.

Having returned to struggle with Eisenstadt's From Generation to Generation *(1956) many times, I cannot recommend it to any but the most intellectually determined. Mannheim's classic 'Essay on Generation' in his* Essays on the Sociology of Knowledge *(1952) has, by contrast, the merit of being relatively short.*

11

Activity

Student-produced questionnaires, aimed at surveying the attitudes and behaviour of different generations, can provide useful research experience and produce findings that will stimulate discussion.

Table 2 *Eight stages of psycho-social development*

stages	psycho-social crises	significant social relations	favourable outcome
1 first year of life	trust versus mistrust	mother or mother substitute	trust and optimism
2 second year	autonomy versus doubt	parents	sense of self-control and adequacy
3 third through fifth years	initiative versus guilt	basic family	purpose and direction; ability to initiate one's own activities
4 sixth year to puberty	industry versus inferiority	neighbourhood; school	competence in intellectual, social, and physical skills
5 adolescence	identity versus confusion	peer groups and outgroups; models of leadership	an integrated image of oneself as a unique person
6 early adulthood	intimacy versus isolation	partners in friendship; sex, competition, co-operation	ability to form close and lasting relationships; to make career commitments
7 middle adulthood	generativity versus self-absorption	divided labour and shared household	concern for family, society, and future generations
8 the ageing years	integrity versus despair	'mankind'; 'my kind'	a sense of fulfilment and satisfaction with one's life; willingness to face death

Source: Erickson (1963), modified in Hilgard (1979: 95).

2

The social construction of childhood and youth

Sociology alone cannot fully explain the experiences of childhood and youth: reference must also be made to biology and psychology. The classic writers on age and generation appreciated biology's contribution to the study of the area, with Eisenstadt, for instance, proposing that 'the basic biological processes are probably more or less similar in all human societies' (Eisenstadt 1956).

Eisenstadt went on to say that 'In every human society this biological process of transition through different age stages, the process of growing up and of ageing, is subject to cultural definitions.' The psychologist Erik Erickson would agree that individual maturation and development must be understood within the cultural context in which it occurs. Although cultural contexts vary, of course, he argued that the eight psycho-social crises presented in Chapter 1 occur in all cultures, and gave the following reason for believing this: 'Each successive stage and crisis has a special relation to one of the basic elements of society, and this for the simple reason that the human life-cycle and man's institutions have evolved together.' (For this link, see columns 2 and 3 of his model, as shown in *Table 2*.) However that may be, Erickson's own cross-cultural studies of childhood and of the life-cycle in general have supported his view. Writing of the eighth psycho-social crisis, integrity (a sense of personal wholeness) versus despair, he suggests 'that a wise Indian, a true gentleman, and a mature peasant share and recognize in one another the final stage of integrity' even though the 'particular style of integrity' may vary according to 'historical place'. (For a critique of Erickson's model, see Chapter 7, pp. 130–34.)

The social construction of childhood

Comparative and historical studies show a variety of perceptions of the stages we refer to as childhood and adolescence.

Comparative perspective

We might expect simple societies to provide the most radically different cultural perceptions of childhood from modern societies. Dr Ruth Benedict, who generally emphasizes the role of culture in forming behaviour, discovers this to be the case (Benedict 1934). She finds broad differences in the way children are treated in simple and modern societies in responsibility/non-responsibility, dominance/submission, and sexual roles. Although Benedict draws her evidence from a number of studies, it is possible to illustrate all three areas from Malinowski's famous study of the Trobriand Islanders.

On the matter of responsibility/non-responsibility, Malinowski says this:

'If the children make up their minds to do a certain thing, to go for a day's expedition, for instance, the grown-ups and even the chief himself, as I often observed, will not be able to

14

stop them. In my ethnographic work I was able and was indeed forced to collect my information about children and their concerns directly from them. Their spiritual ownership in games and childish activities was acknowledged, and they were also quite capable of instructing me and explaining the intricacies of their play or enterprise.'

(Malinowski 1957: 45–6)

Trobriand children learn tribal tradition and custom through imitation and communication rather than authority. Women in Trobriand society have substantial control and autonomy in certain areas and, according to Malinowski, there is less tension in the nuclear family as a result. Authority is exercised mainly from outside the nuclear unit, by the mother's brother who is the male head of the family. Although he genuinely enforces law and other constraints, he normally lives at some distance from the child, sometimes even in another village, and his authority only comes into play from about the child's sixth year. Relieved of much of his function as enforcer of authority, the father is freed to become much more of a friend and guide to his children.

We now consider dominance/submission. The above discussion already indicates that relations between children and adults in Trobriand society (involving dominance/submission) are different from those in modern societies. It is worth dwelling again on the relationship of the father to the child which Malinowski describes as 'near friend and helper'. He goes on to say that: 'At the time when our father makes himself pleasant at best by his entire absence from the nursery, the Trobriand father is first a nurse and then a companion.' Malinowski was writing of the role of father in the west in the 1920s, and although it is now probably less authoritarian, it is still hardly that of 'a nurse and then a companion'.

Benedict's third point of comparison is sexual roles. I will not analyse male/female sexual roles in detail but make a general point. Such is the degree of sexual freedom among children in

Trobriand society that it is likely to cause shock to many in our supposedly permissive culture. Malinowski writes:

'They indulge in plays and pastimes in which they satisfy their curiosity concerning the appearance and function of the organs of generation, and incidentally receive, it would seem, a certain amount of positive pleasure. Genital manipulation and such minor perversions as oral stimulation of the organs are typical forms of this amusement.'

(Malinowski 1957: 47)

Adults responded to this with 'tolerance and amused interest' and 'easy jocularity'.

It is important to note that Trobriand society is not typical of simple societies, nor are Benedict's three points universal to them. Precise cultural practices depend upon particular conditions and we must be cautious of generalizations. That, really, is the point. 'Childhood' is quite different in some societies than in our own.

Historical perspective

In *Centuries of Childhood* (1962), Philippe Ariès provides an historical account of the origins of the 'idea of childhood' in western Europe. He argues: 'In medieval society the idea of childhood did not exist.' He sees 'a connection between the idea of childhood and the idea of the family', both of which began to emerge during the fifteenth century. By this he means that the unique importance attached to the family in modern society goes hand in hand with child-centredness. In the middle ages emphasis was not on the family but on 'community' and 'sociability'. Ariès makes much of the fact that his examination of medieval icons frequently showed large groups or 'crowds' depicted, but rarely families or children. Indeed, he says that medieval iconographers were unable to depict children other than as young adults. In medieval society a dependent stage of infancy was, of course, recognized but once s/he 'had passed the age of five or seven, the child was immediately absorbed into the world of adults'.

Ariès finds that two concepts of childhood developed from the fifteenth century, particularly among the upper and middle classes. The first was characterized by 'coddling', in which the child, 'on account of his sweetness, simplicity, and drollery, became a source of amusement and relaxation for the adult'. It was from about this time that the upper class began to dress their children in special clothes. The second concept, popularized by the clergy, was of the child as a 'fragile creature of God'. Partly because of the clergy's keenness to save young souls, schools began more and more to specialize in the education of the young, whereas previously adults had also attended freely. To summarize, Ariès's view is that the 'family and school together removed the child from adult society'.

Ariès shows an acute awareness of class as well as age stratification and, in fact, in his account of the emergence of the idea of childhood, links the two together. Initially, the concept of childhood flourished among the upper class. However, the cultivation of childhood was practised by the rising bourgeoisie following the industrial and commercial expansion of the eighteenth century. Increasingly, middle-class children received lengthy educations, in France in the lycées, and in England in the public schools. Lower-class children at this time were still expected to work, and the pattern of their lives was much closer to the medieval one describes by Ariès. However, he does observe some stratified diffusion (or spread) of middle-class attitudes to children to the working class. On the matter of age and class, Ariès comments: 'There is accordingly a remarkable synchronism between the modern age group and the social (class) group: both originated at the same time, in the late eighteenth century, and in the same milieu – the middle class.'

Industrialization, then, is the underlying factor behind the development of the privatized, child-centred family. Ariès is not enthusiastic about the modern family or modern society:

17

'everywhere it (industrialization) reinforced private life at the expense of neighbourly relationships, friendships, and traditional contacts.' He remarks almost complainingly that: 'The problem of the transmission of property takes second place to that of the children's welfare.' Because the family no longer produces as a unit, it is not linked with the larger community through work and leisure. Women and children are not generally required in the main economy and women find their major role in child (and husband) care.

Ariès's work is complex and original, and has found its way into standard sociological textbooks with little critical evaluation. However, it is open to a number of qualifications. First, it is characterized by a nostalgia for the past, and particularly for 'lost community'. Thus in comparing individuality in the medieval and modern periods he asks rhetorically: 'Was there not greater individuality in the gay indifference of the prolific fathers of the *ancien régime*?' The 'indifference of the prolific fathers' to which he is referring is to children. Indeed, there are points in Ariès's book when one wonders if he likes children at all – it is rather as if he thinks they 'should be seen and not heard'. His tendency to romanticize supposed pre-industrial community opens him up to the criticisms frequently made against the *gemeinschaft/ gesellschaft* (community/association) school, of whom Tönnies was the original representative. What they and Ariès tend to overlook are the conflicts and inequalities of pre-industrial times.

The second point of criticism is related to the first. Ariès's comparison of the situation of medieval and modern children disproportionately favours the earlier period. Thus he writes rather irascibly that 'Our world is obsessed by the physical, moral, and sexual problems of children' and comments that, in medieval civilization, at about seven years old the child 'became the natural companion of the adult'. It is on precisely this point that Lloyd de Mause disagrees with Ariès. He finds substantial evidence that children were often brutally treated in pre-modern times and that matters are now much improved.

18

In this sense he describes his 'central thesis' as the 'opposite' of that of Ariès (de Mause 1976).

Contemporary issues: childhood, motherhood, the state, and inequality

Whatever view one takes of Ariès and his critics, there is no doubt that he is right that in the modern family women have usually borne the immediate burden of caring for children. That this is still the case is shown in *The Social Life of Britain's Five Year Olds*, a report by the Child Health and Education Survey (Osborn, Butler, and Morris 1984). The report is based on responses by parents and health visitors to questionnaires about 13,135 children who were five in the second week of April 1975, the year the survey was carried out. Reviewing the report, Caroline St John-Brooks says:

'The report is, of course, focused on the lives of children. But the lives of their mothers actually emerge from it with extra clarity. Mothers are still by far the most important people in their five year olds' lives. The "symmetrical family" … is hard to find.

Quite rightly, it is noted that many women find mothering interesting and stimulating as well as hard work. But the mothers' answers to the questionnaire on maternal depression make disheartening reading. Over half "often get worried about things", nearly half are "easily irritated and upset", a third often have bad headaches, a third often have backache, a third often feel miserable or depressed, a third feel tired most of the time.

Assuming that the same third of the sample is not answering "Yes" all the time, it's a picture of pretty widespread malaise and exhaustion. And fathers do astonishingly little to help.' (St John-Brooks 1984: 262)

The role of the modern state in legislating for the welfare of the child needs to be noted. It has increased greatly in the last century. Partly, the state generally supports the family, as in the provision of child allowances. The universal availability of state education from the age of five is perhaps the major expression of state concern and involvement in child welfare. The state also makes alternative provisions for children when the family fails to cope. Under the banner of children's rights, the state has gradually eroded the power of parents over their children. In certain circumstances the local authority can take a child 'into care', even against the wishes of the parents. There are currently over 100,000 children in care. Current opinions tends to be unenthusiastic about institutionalized care. Since the 1960s the view that the needy child's natural family should be supported as far as possible to enable it to keep the child has also waned in popularity. Fostering is now more widely favoured, a policy which seems to put the principle of practical care above that of natural family relationships. The trend towards substitute care increased following the 1975 Children's Act.

In a society in which a substantial minority of marriages break down, state protection for the child provides a necessary safety net. Partly with the increasing role of the state in mind, Halsey, Heath, and Ridge (1980) goes so far as to suggest 'a weakening of the bond between parent and child' in 'the so-called century of the child'. However, Ronald Fletcher's (1966) view that *both* state and parents are now more intensely involved in the socialization and welfare of the child is also arguable.

Finally, the sheer variety of social circumstances experienced by children is noteworthy. The most important factor of all is social class – a point highlighted in the Child Health and Education Survey. There is also great variation in childhood among different ethnic groups and this, of course, affects how children relate to the dominant culture (see Chapter 4). The extremes of advantage and disadvantage experienced by children, and the resulting inequalities of opportunity, are too familiar to need repeating here but their importance cannot be overemphasized. 'Problems' occur more frequently in poor families. A 'family policy' aimed at eradicating poverty might be more effective than dealing with the 'symptoms' or 'problems' poverty helps to produce.

Activities

1 How does the use of comparative and historical material help to illustrate 'the social construction of childhood'?

2 What are the advantages and disadvantages of the modern, 'child-centred' family? (Reference to chapters on the family and gender in standard sociology textbooks will be useful in answering this question.

The social construction of youth

Comparative perspective

In the case of youth, comparative and historical approaches again illustrate the variety of social perspectives on the life cycle. For the sake of continuity, I shall use Malinowski's Trobriand research (1957) for comparative purposes and Ariès's *Centuries of Childhood* (1962), which also deals with the emergence of 'modern' adolescence, for historical reference. I shall also refer to Margaret Mead's famous, or perhaps now infamous, study *Coming of Age in Samoa* (1971). However, since Derek Freeman's (1983) scholarly efforts to expose Mead's Samoan findings as 'an anthropological myth', we can no longer treat them as reliable. Apart from the methodological issues, Mead's study and Freeman's refutation of it can be regarded as significant episodes in the debate about the relative importance of biological and cultural factors in explaining behaviour, including that of youth.

Malinowski: adolescence among the Trobriand Islanders
According to Malinowski, adolescence among the Trobrianders is a period of transition, as it is in the west, but it is structured by very different cultural norms and assumptions. I shall briefly present Malinowski's analysis of the development

21

of work and sex roles among Trobriand youth. On the matter of preparation for work, he writes:

'(Adolescents) are so far not claimed by any serious duties, yet their greater physical strength and ripeness give them more independence and a wider scope of action than they had as children. The adolescent boys participate, but mainly as freelances, in garden work .... in the fishing and hunting in overseas expeditions; they get all the excitement and pleasure, as well as some of the prestige, yet remain free from a great deal of the drudgery and many of the restrictions which trammel and weigh on their elders. Many of the taboos are not yet quite binding on them, the burden of magic has not yet fallen on their shoulders. If they grow tired of work, they simply stop and rest ....

Girls, too, obtain a certain amount of the enjoyment and excitement denied to children by joining in some of the activities of their elders, whilst still escaping the worst of the drudgery.'   (Malinowski 1957: 55)

According to Malinowski, Trobriand 'adolescence marks the transition between infantile and playful sexualities and those serious permanent relations which precede marriage. During this intermediate period love becomes passionate yet remains free.' For us, then, Trobriand adolescent sexual behaviour presents the paradox that a future marriage partner is sought and yet, even after s/he has been found, the freedom to have other, occasional sexual relations remains. This even extends to participating in ritual orgies in which one sex has fairly free access to the other and which may involve a group of males or females visiting a neighbouring village to take part. Even when marriage actually approaches, temporary liaisons may legitimately occur, though not after marriage.

A feature of adolescent life among the Trobrianders is the institution of the *bukumatula*, or 'house for bachelors', to which they might invite unmarried girls. A number of couples would live in one of these houses forming a temporary community, although individual couples would be given the

22

opportunity of privacy. Malinowski noted that the influence of missionaries had caused the number of bachelors' establishments to dwindle which in his view would 'not enhance true sex morality.'

Malinowski shares with the functionalist Eisenstadt an emphasis on the transitional nature of adolescence in most simple as well as modern societies. However, he stresses how much the cultural framework and details vary. A major variation from many societies is the greater degree of informality and freedom in the areas of both work preparation and courtship in Trobriand society. Malinowski explains this in terms of the generally less authoritarian nature of Trobriand society compared to, for instance, that of inter-war Britain (the period when he was writing). In turn, he links this liberality to the strong influence of women in Trobriand society. However, he does not go as far as those (mainly Marxists) who consider that capitalism and patriarchy combine to produce a social system that is both economically and sexually repressive in Britain and similar societies. Later, however, the Freudian-Marxist, Wilhelm Reich, used Malinowski's work to argue that the communal and 'feminist' principles of social organization practised by the Trobrianders were freer and less repressive than those of the capitalist and patriarchal west.

Derek Freeman's critique of Margaret Mead   Until recently, Margaret Mead's *Coming of Age in Samoa*, originally published in 1928, was widely considered to be a major contribution to the biology versus culture debate. This was exactly what she intended it to be:

'And through this description I have tried to answer the question which sent me to Samoa: are the disturbances which vex our adolescents due to the nature of adolescence itself or to the civilization? Under different conditions does adolescence present a different picture?'   (Mead 1971: 17)

Mead believed that her observations provided convincing refutation of the view that adolescence is universally and innately 'problematic' – she thought she had found a crucial

23

'negative instance' (contradictory case). Her study focused mainly on fifty girls in three small neighbouring villages, though to help her do this more effectively she also attempted to examine the social life of the area as a whole. This is what she concluded about the girls, to which there were only a few exceptions:

'Adolescence represented no period of crisis or stress, but was instead an orderly developing of a set of slowly maturing interests and activities. The girls' minds were perplexed by no conflicts, troubled by no philosophical queries, beset by no remote ambitions. To live as a girl with many lovers as long as possible and then to marry in one's own village, near one's own relatives, and to have many children, these were uniform and satisfying ambitions.'

(Mead 1971: 129)

I shall illustrate Freeman's fundamental disagreement with this picture by reference to two major areas: sexual behaviour and delinquency (Freeman 1983). Mead acknowledged a traditional respect for pre-marital virginity among females in Samoa but, as the above quotation shows, considered that it was widely disregarded. She even implied that women of high rank, including the highest, the *tapou*, whose virginity was heavily guarded by her kin, not infrequently evaded the system, sometimes by temporary elopement. Freeman, however, cites extensive evidence to show that 'virtually every family cherishes the virginity of its daughters', and that a robust system of protection and surveillance was mounted by a girl's brothers 'whatever her rank'. To demonstrate his case, he gives a number of examples of painful retribution exacted upon those who sought to break propriety. Perhaps Freeman's most telling point is his simple reinterpretation of Mead's own data on the virginity of a group of twenty-five girls. She lists thirteen of these as having had no heterosexual experience, a fact which Freeman finds 'obviously incongruent with her generalizations about Samoan female adolescents'.

24

Freeman also tackles Mead on her own ground on the issue of delinquency. In the group of twenty-five girls from whom she draws most of her data, Mead mentions three as delinquent; Freeman adds a fourth, who had breached the incest taboo but whom 'Mead inexplicably did not even class as deviant'. Freeman then compares the delinquency rate in this group with that for females in England and Wales (in 1965). The rate for the Samoan group was ten times higher! Freeman recognizes the approximate nature of his comparison but considers it indicates that the rate of delinquency among the girls studied by Mead in 1925–26 'was in fact at quite a high level'. In addition to the four delinquents, Mead also found three 'upward deviants' in the group – girls who had aspirations at variance with those expected by their kin. As Freeman says, together these 'make up 28 per cent of her sample of twenty-five female adolescents (who) are obviously every bit as much a product of the Samoan social environment as are the eighteen other adolescent girls who were, Mead tells us, untroubled and unstressed'.

In summary, Freeman makes two major points. First, as a piece of evidence about the role of culture in structuring adolescent experience, *Coming of Age in Samoa* must be treated with the utmost scepticism. Not to mince words, Freeman states that Mead's account is 'fundamentally in error'. Second, he makes a general methodological point. He supports Karl Popper in advocating that researchers should attempt to disprove or 'falsify' their own hypothesis. This is more rigorous than trying to prove it. Clearly, Mead did not adopt this approach and Freeman argues that her commitment to a belief in the strong formative power of culture prevented her from achieving rational and impartial analysis.

Historical perspective

We can again use Philippe Ariès's *Centuries of Childhood* (1962) to provide an historical perspective on the social construction of an age group, in this case youth. The separating-off of youth was at first an upper- and middle-class phenomenon, and occurred mainly in the schools. The family as such played a less important part in the formation of youth than of childhood. The process of a separate and highly disciplined education for the well-to-do culminated in what Ariès refers to as the 'claustrophobic boarding school' of the eighteenth and nineteenth centuries, of which *Tom Brown's Schooldays* is the classic fictional account. The arrival of mass education in the latter part of the nineteenth century contributed to the growth of age groups among working-class youth. Similarly, the expansion of the higher education system in the twentieth century gave mainly middle-class youth a shared collective experience and identity. Ariès also attributes considerable importance to the adoption of large-scale conscription from the late eighteenth century in sharpening awareness of adolescence as a distinct age stage. This factor was particularly important during the First World War, which generated a sense of collective identity among servicemen. However, the role of the educational system is surely of longer-term and more fundamental importance in structuring adolescent experience, and I shall examine it further in the next section.

Activity

Write an essay or have a group discussion on the implications that Freeman's critique of Margaret Mead's *Coming of Age in Samoa* has for the biology/culture debate on adolescence.

Is there a modern youth culture?

Almost no sociologist now believes that a general youth culture exists in the sense that a majority of young people share the same 'way of life'. As early as the 1920s Karl Mannheim coined the term 'generational unit' to describe the fact that different groups within the same generation acquired distinct identities. Today we know such factors as class and race cut across youth, and help to produce a variety of youth subcultures (see Chapters 3 and 4).

Although there is no universal youth culture, two elements in modern society affect nearly all young people in one way or another. These are (1) compulsory education, and (2) the relative affluence of modern youth in relation to the consumer goods industry. These factors provide no more than a framework for understanding modern youth; detailed analysis concentrates on the varying extent and manner by which different groups of young people are affected. Quite evidently, for instance, not all young people are equally affluent, and some are not affluent at all.

The educational system in industrial society

The industrial revolution generated the socio-economic context in which modern youth developed. The educational system grew more or less parallel with economic expansion, providing the immediate institutional environment in which youth began to take shape, rather as the factory system did for the working class. Sociologists tend to stress two fundamental reasons for the growth of the educational system. First, functionalists (such as Eisenstadt) emphasize that basic education and training are necessary in an industrial society. At the minimum, people need an elementary competence in the three 'r's' to function adequately. Thus the 1880 Education Act introduced a system of compulsory universal education (to the age of ten) in Britain for the first time. The minimum school-leaving age is now sixteen, but a majority of young people have some further education or formal training after that.

Second, sociologists agree that education plays an important part in the socialization and social control of youth, though they differ in their interpretations of this. Whereas functionalists regard these 'functions' as necessary for social order, conflict theorists tend to see them as 'processes' beneficial to capitalism but not always to youth itself. Harry Braverman, a

Marxist, has argued that schools serve a major 'child-minding' function in modern societies, which releases adult female labour onto the employment market. Braverman (1974) and Berg (1970) regard these considerations as more important in explaining the growth of the education system than the need for training. They recognize the necessity of basic education, particularly in science and technology. However, they do not regard the proliferation of qualifications in advanced capitalist societies as generally economically useful, rather they see it as a mechanism of social control. Largely unwanted on the employment market, young people occupy their energies pursuing qualifications, many of which are inherently useless. Berg's research suggests that the increasing numbers of people overqualified for their jobs tend to work less effectively than those appropriately qualified. Berg and Braverman recognize that qualifications carry weight in the employment market but they would agree with Bowles and Gintis (1976) that the underlying mechanism for occupational selection is social class and, I would add, the state of the employment market itself. There is no future in being qualified for a job that is not there! The interaction of the educational system with class, race, and gender factors will be analysed in Chapters 3 and 4. Eton and 'Bash Street', of course, tell us a different story.

Affluence and the consumer industry

The second factor (or rather two related factors) referred to above is the relative affluence of modern youth in relation to the consumer goods industry. Again, this is a product of industrialized society. Teenage affluence is most obvious in advanced capitalist countries, but it is also becoming apparent among sections of Soviet youth. Mark Abrams's pamphlet 'The Teenage Consumer' (1959) was one of the first major analyses of this issue. Abrams demonstrated that teenage prosperity was a postwar development. He defined teenage as 'a collective word describing young people from the time they leave school till they either marry or reach twenty-five'.

Between 1938 and 1958 the real earnings of young people increased 50 per cent, double that of adults. Significantly, their *uncommitted* income (i.e. what remained after necessities had been met) probably increased by about 100 per cent. Teenage spending as a percentage of all consumer spending in 1957 was 6.3 per cent, but in certain areas it was very much more (see *Table 3*). It is the size of teenage spending in specific areas that created and still creates a specific teenage market.

Table 3 *Expenditure by teenagers, 1957*

market area	teenage spending as % of all consumer spending
records, record players, etc.	44.1
bicycles, motorcycles, etc.	38.5
other entertainments	30.6
cinema admissions	26.3
cosmetics	24.2
recreational goods	18.8

Source: Abbreviated and adapted from Abrams (1959: 11).

Abrams makes a number of important observations about the new 'teenage economy'. I will mention three of these and add to each comments relevant to the period since Abrams published his article. First, he contrasts the steady, adult-type jobs 1950s teenagers had in the main manufacturing and service sectors with the 'dead-end' occupations they typically had before the Second World War. Thus in 1931 nearly a third of all employed females under twenty-five were engaged in domestic service. In the 1980s, of course, the so-called 'economic facts of life' have changed again, and the young do not easily find employment in either the manufacturing or service sectors.

Second, Abrams found that 'the teenage market is almost entirely working class' (among whom he includes routine white-collar employees). He points out that middle-class teenagers starting either college or a career had less disposable income and, I would suggest, less free time. For the 1950s, at least, Abrams's observations seem correct. The mainly working-class 'teddy boys' were perhaps the first example of a postwar youth subculture. They certainly flaunted their relative wealth and partly adopted the style and, less expertly, some of the affectations of upper-class 'toffs'. On the other hand, they had a full measure of the toughness and aggression characteristic of nearly all working-class youth subcultures. I will examine some of these in more detail early in Chapter 3.

It is safe to generalize that the youth consumer market expanded further during the 1960s and beyond, although it probably began to contract in the early 1980s. The first reason for this expansion was a demographic one and was, in fact, projected by Abrams himself. Because of the postwar 'baby boom', the number of teenagers increased during the 1960s by about 20 per cent. Second, the 'affluence' factor became even more pronounced in the 1960s. Middle-class teenagers may have consumed less conspicuously than their working-class counterparts, but consume they did. Even so, in the early 1960s it was the styles of the predominantly working-class 'mods' and 'rockers' that caught the public eye. However, by the end of the 1960s, Abrams's comment that 'the aesthetic of the teenage market is essentially ... working class' was no longer true. The fashion hype of the late 1960s onwards did not distinguish between the money of working-class and middle-class youth, and the match between style and class, always ambiguous, became highly fluid.

Abrams makes a third observation, that young males dominated the teenage market. They accounted for 67 per cent of teenage spending, and though the disparity is now less when young people first enter the job market, it is still substantial by the time they are in their mid-twenties. This factor can be taken to represent the general dominance of males in youth 'culture' and British society as a whole, and is a theme to which I shall return frequently.

Before commenting on Abrams's influential article, I shall broaden the discussion of teenage affluence and consumption by introducing two major themes of postwar social analysis: first, the development of 'mass society' and a corresponding supposed decline of the working class (particularly working-class 'militancy'); second, the influence of the United States on British culture, and specifically teenage culture.

Mass society theory argued that an expanding, affluent middle section of British society had developed, comprising well-paid manual workers and increasing numbers of comfortably-off white-collar employees. This group provided the bulk of the market for capitalist mass production. It was argued that because most of the working class shared in this economic success story, its commitment to radical, let alone revolutionary, change had been diluted. A different way of interpreting these socio-economic trends was embourgeoisement theory, which argued that the skilled working class was becoming 'more middle class' in its economic, social, and political behaviour. Goldthorpe and Lockwood (1969) tested this thesis and concluded it was too simplistic, but they did find strong currents of convergence between their samples of skilled working- and lower middle-class employees. In particular, both groups typically viewed work instrumentally (i.e. mainly as a means of making money), and their consumption and life style were mainly family based. Goldthorpe's and Lockwood's sample was of married men. However, it seems safe to assume highly instrumental attitudes to work on the part of working- and middle-class teenagers also. They, of course, channelled their income into supporting their particular patterns of consumption and life style.

There was a political aspect to this picture of contentment. Although not a mass society theorist, Ralf Dahrendorf argued in *Class and Class Conflict in Industrial Society* (1959) that class conflict had become 'institutionalized' in what he called 'post-capitalist' society and that little possibility of, and no good reason for, revolution remained. The 'institutionalization' he referred to was the development of the trade union

31

movement and the Labour Party as the major vehicles for the expression of working-class interests. These institutions now played a legitimate part within 'liberal democracy'. He believed that a broad consensus had been established, reflecting the fundamentals of liberal democracy: a mixed economy, a welfare state, and representative democracy. In the 1960s this basic consensus – assumed or real – was much stressed by social commentators and politicians alike. The implication was that now there existed agreement on fundamentals, people could get on with living 'the good life'.

The second theme, the influence of the United States on British culture, is related to the first. Mass society theory was even more influential in the United States than in Britain. This is not surprising in view of the popular, though I would argue erroneous, notion among Americans that the United States is a classless society. An alternative framework to class analysis is elite/mass theory, which simply sees a two-fold division of society. The radical left-wing sociologist, Charles Wright Mills, and the liberal functionalist, Edward Shils, both employed this perspective. For many Britons the concept of mass society was remote but they were open to the influence of American culture, particularly in its brashest and most commercial forms. Although American television and cinema films and pop records were avidly consumed, popular expressions of resentment against American influence also occurred. Perhaps this ambivalence reflected affronted nationalism – a sense that Britain in decline was making way for America in the ascendant.

The commercial mass media was the means which made possible the 'explosion' of youth in the mid-1950s and early 1960s. If the 'explosion' did not begin in America, then that is certainly where the energy and impetus were strongest initially. Money and youthful energy were the driving forces, though they were not always possessed by the same people. The postwar American youth market was huge and the leisure industry was soon competing for its favours. The American-produced film *The Blackboard Jungle* is often thought of as the symbolic beginning of 'modern youth culture'. It starred Bill Hayley and his Comets, who preceded Elvis Presley in introducing rock 'n roll into Britain. The film and its major hit song, 'Rock Around the Clock', made millions, but commercial success or not it released some very genuine feelings among American and British youth. As Ray Gosling says, in his BBC radio broadcast recounting postwar youth culture: 'We went ape and bananas ... we stood on our bucket seats and hollered.' And Gosling a grammar school boy, too! It was mainly working-class youth who first got caught up in rock 'n roll in Britain, but Gosling wasn't the only middle-class youth to switch his college uniform for drainpipes and the rest of the 'ted gear'.

In the United States the high school and even college systems did not reflect class divisions as sharply as did the grammar/secondary modern system in England and Wales. This and the generally higher level of disposable income among American youth encouraged the mass market approach of the media, fashion, and leisure industries. But because producers may treat young people as a 'mass' does not mean that they behave as a mass. Closer examination shows that American, like British, youth differentiate themselves along class, ethnic, and other lines. Indeed, the history of postwar youth is largely about the interaction and tension between the forces of conformity generated by mass production and the frequently nonconformist creativity of at least some young people.

Once the impetus had been established, the music and films began to pour in. Pop stars like Gene Vincent and Eddie Cochran, and film stars such as James Dean and Marlon Brando made vulnerable, brooding heroes – 'just like us' – except that they actually did become millionaires overnight. Britain's entertainment industry soon produced its own 'stars'. Tommy Steele, Cliff Richard, and Adam Faith vied with the American singers. They all made films, too, and even if their acting was a little wooden, they and their backers could still account themselves successful – in money terms.

Still, commercially packaged though their offerings were, something vital and even rebellious came through at a high level of decibels.

We can now return to Abrams's comments on 1950s youth with reference to the broader context and debate discussed above. By 1964 Abrams had followed the logic of his earlier arguments and declared in *The Newspaper Reading Public of Tomorrow* that differences in age had become more relevant for study than those of social class. The former were increasing and the latter decreasing. As we have seen, he defined the boundaries of age groups by differences in market position. Thus in 1959 he sharply delineated the division between teenager and married adult: 'On marrying the teenager starts almost from scratch to learn the consuming habits appropriate to the new role.'

A number of American sociologists have argued that a youth culture exists along the lines suggested by Abrams. One of the best-known presentations of this case is given in Peter and Brigitte Berger's *Sociology: A Biographical Approach* (1976), where they refer to 'the mass character of modern youth'. Succinctly, they note 'quantitative' and 'qualitative' aspects to this. The quantitative factors are that in modern society advances in medicine and hygiene ensure that more young people survive than in the past; and they have a mass presence in the educational system. Qualitatively, they believe that in life style and attitude 'to a considerable degree, the youth culture cuts across class lines'. They adopt Tom Wolfe's term 'status spheres' to describe these cross-class youth groupings. More than Abrams, Berger and Berger retain a class perspective in analysing youth but, as the following passage shows, this is blurred by the superimposition of the concept of a youth culture which crosses class lines:

'It is also important to understand the relation of the youth culture to the stratification system. To a considerable degree, the youth culture cuts across class lines. To take up once more Tom Wolfe's helpful term of "status spheres", the youth culture has created symbols and patterns of behaviour

34

that are capable of bestowing status upon individuals coming from quite different class backgrounds. In addition, as part of its morality of relentless sincerity (not to say nudity), the youth culture has a strongly egalitarian ethos which has not only made it a locale of quite remarkable racial tolerance but in a real way a kind of classless society. This obliteration of class lines is especially marked in the external manifestations of the subculture. Thus young people of all classes can participate in the collective ecstasies of a rock festival (and, as far as is known, this is what actually takes place on these occasions). Class lines begin to be more important when it comes to consumption patterns, since young people of different classes have different amounts of money to spend. We have already referred to the considerable expense involved in obtaining adequate equipment for the reproduction of youth music; not everyone, after all, can afford a top hi-fi system.'

(Berger and Berger 1976: 251–52)

Berger's and Berger's emphasis on youth culture as characterized by open-status systems may have been affected by events occurring at the time they were writing – in the late 1960s and very early 1970s. The American youth movement was then at its height and perhaps seemed more generally influential than it does in retrospect. Berger and Berger were well aware that this was a middle-class led movement, and they qualify the above analysis accordingly. I return to this matter fully in Chapter 5.

I will now offer some criticisms of Abrams's position, which to some extent are also applicable to Berger and Berger, and then conclude this section with an overall appraisal of it.

First, Abrams was wholly uncritical of capitalism, either in its economic or cultural aspects. Perhaps he saw himself simply as a market researcher whose job was to report facts and trends. As a result major aspects of the mass society debate pass him by. This debate ranged over issues of quality and taste in consumption, and over the control and manipulation of the market and media. Radicals like C. Wright Mills and Herbert

Marcuse, liberals such as Vance Packard and David Riesman, agonized over the excessive conformity and artificial contentment that they associated with mass society. Abrams's work seems to require a more explicit stance on these matters.

Second, Abrams underestimates the extent of continuing class divisions and the resulting inequalities. Race he wrote little about. As might be expected of a male writing in the 1950s his treatment of gender now seems inadequate. Yet it is within the structures of class, race, and gender that youth must be understood. During the 1960s and 1970s these fundamental divisions in British (and American) society were widely explored by social critics. Michael Harrington (1962) rediscovered 'the other America' of poverty and lack of opportunity. Peter Townsend (1979) did the same in Britain. The urban disorders in America in the mid-1960s put the issue of racial conflict onto the British political agenda as well. In retrospect, the women's movement has perhaps challenged existing attitudes more widely and effectively than any other. Awareness of these developments has profoundly influenced analysis of youth. In concentrating so much on what he saw as a global youth market (in which he, admittedly, perceived the young, working-class male as the leading consumer), Abrams missed the emergence of specific youth subcultures which fully reflected class, race, and gender factors. I will present work that does reflect these factors, including that of the Centre for Contemporary Cultural Studies (CCCS), in Chapters 3 and 4 which can, therefore, be read as an extended critique of the 'youth culture' perspective.

Despite its limitations, Abrams's work does draw attention to real developments in the capitalist socio-economic system. The British people in the 1950s, including most of the working class, were much wealthier than in the 1930s, just as today they are substantially wealthier than in the 1950s. Young people had a relatively large share of this wealth. Abrams is also right in observing the growth of a mass youth market. This does not mean that all young people buy the same things, but that the same things are there for all to buy. Particular styles in clothes or music may begin at the grass roots, but a whole commercial system stands ready to package them for 'the mass'. In Britain and America there is always a chance that you will turn a corner and bump into someone carbon-copying your own 'unique' style. Only the very rich or the home-sewers can escape this. In a relatively affluent society differences in income, other than at the extreme, do not prevent mass trends in consumption developing. Despite this, the size and wealth of the teenage consumer market has recently encouraged manufacturers to cater for a variety of tastes. The wealthier the total teenage market, the more this tendency can be pursued.

Abrams overestimated the decline of class in Britain, but he did successfully indicate that trends in production and consumption might reduce working-class militancy, and highlight generational differences. Although Abrams has frequently been criticized by socialists, by 1984 many members of the Labour Party had decided that the relative affluence of *sections* of the working class was a reality they needed to accept and accommodate. However, the divisions of class and race continued to affect young people, structuring their experience of youth very differently. An adequate analysis of youth, therefore, needs to explain how young people, from their different structural positions in society, variously respond to the forces of capitalism, including those described by Abrams. Some conform, more or less, but many do not. Certainly, the differences between young people are too great to speak of a single 'youth culture', despite the efforts of producers to create a mass teenage market.

'Ordinary' youth: functionalist perspective and social survey data

The major points of functionalist theory on youth have been referred to in analysing Eisenstadt (1956), but it will be helpful to summarize them here and link youth cultural and functionalist theory.

First, both Eisenstadt and his mentor, Talcott Parsons, see

modern youth as a stage of *transition* from family roles (characterized by affectivity, diffuseness, particularism, ascription, and collectivity orientation) to adult roles (characterized by affective neutrality, specificity, universalism, achievement, and self-orientation). To help accomplish this transition, formal agencies of secondary socialization exist, such as schools and youth organizations, but informal peer groups also contribute (see the third point below). Second, youth, because it is a period of training and preparation, is of lower status and power than adulthood. Functionalists recognize that the marginal status of and the 'constraints' on youth can cause inter-generational friction, but they have tended to examine the functions rather than the dysfunctions of youth. Eisenstadt appreciated that 'lower-class' boys did not always 'fit in to' the social system, but this insight has been pursued much more fully by both American and British subcultural theorists (see Chapter 3).

Third, functionalists stress the functions of the peer group in providing status, identity, room for role experimentation, the opportunity for play (continuing childhood needs), and to make relationships. Frank Musgrove (1964) summarizes a body of research done as far afield as Britain, Australia, and the United States which suggests that the larger peer group ('crowd') and smaller friendship group ('clique') are virtually universal (the latter particularly among girls). Youth culture fulfils the same range of functions as the peer group. Indeed, youth culture is peer group activity. (Functionalists offer little analysis of the commercial production of 'youth culture'.) Despite things 'occasionally getting out of hand', the peer group is generally regarded as a successful means of secondary socialization. Similarly, youth culture may sometimes run to excess but even this acts as a safety valve for childish, unsocialized, and deviant activity. In time, most young people 'grow up and conform'.

From young people's own point of view, youth culture enables them to work through many of the problems of 'transition' without seriously confronting older, more powerful generations (though it may not always seem that way!). Quentin Crisp is no sociologist but an acute observer of the social scene. Inadvertently, no doubt, there is a functional-ist smack about his pithy summary of the paradox of youth and the manner of its solution: 'The young have always the same problem: how to rebel and how to conform at the same time. They've solved this by rebelling against their elders and copying each other' (Crisp 1981). Not quite, of course, but the grain of truth is there. In fact, social surveys on the attitudes and behaviour of youth consistently show that young people consider that they get on well with their parents, though rather less so with teachers (see, for instance, National Children's Bureau (1976)). Revealingly, however, such disagreements as occur tend to focus on issues of style (e.g. length or colour of hair) or personal freedom (what time to return home from an evening out). Still, the social survey can be a cumbersome tool of enquiry, often missing crucial aspects of class, race, and gender, and such data need cautious interpretation. Neverthe-less *Table 4*, showing generally high levels of satisfaction with life among the youth of the European Community, is fairly typical of the findings of social surveys on youth and is difficult to dismiss out of hand.

The major criticism of functionalist perspective is that it deals inadequately with the impact of all aspects of social stratification on youth – particularly the major ones of class, race, and gender. Chapters 3 and 4 explore these matters in detail. Finally, generalizations about the functions of youth are not always supported by examination of contrary evidence about youth conflict. Karl Popper's enjoinder to test one's own hypothesis by attempting to disprove it is rarely practised by functionalists. Again, we must look elsewhere to explore the dimension of youth conflict.

Activities

1 Why did what Mark Abrams refers to as 'youth culture' appear so prominently in the 1950s?
2 What truth, if any, do you think there is in the quotation from Quentin Crisp towards the end of this chapter?

Table 4 *Satisfaction with life in the ten countries of the Community (all age groups combined)*

	Bel	Den	Ger	Fra	Ire	Italy	Lux	N	UK	Gr	EEC
very satisfied	29	57	20	16	40	14	39	42	36	18	24
fairly satisfied	51	37	63	63	46	57	48	52	50	46	57
not very satisfied	12	5	12	16	11	22	9	4	9	22	14
not at all satisfied	4	—	2	5	2	7	3	1	4	13	4
no reply	4	1	3	—	1	—	1	1	1	1	1
total	100	100	100	100	100	100	100	100	100	100	100
index	3.11	3.52	3.05	2.91	3.26	2.78	3.25	3.37	3.19	2.69	3.0

Note: Mean calculated by applying 4 to the answer 'very satisfied', 3 to 'fairly satisfied', 2 to 'not very satisfied', and 1 to 'not at all satisfied', after excluding 'don't knows/no replies' from the calculation. The central point (2.5) is thus the borderline between satisfaction and dissatisfaction.

Source: Commission of the European Communities (1982: 40).

Further reading

Since the publication of Freeman's book in paperback, it is possible to pursue his critique of Margaret Mead cheaply. The relevant volumes are Mead (1971) and Freeman (1983). On a more contemporary note, the following is a mine of useful information: Osborn, Butler, and Morris, The Social Life of Britain's Five Year Olds *(1984).*

Those who want to explore the origins of the 'youth culture debate' will find it worthwhile to track down the brief but influential pamphlet by Mark Abrams (1959) in a large library. For those who can find a transcript of Ray Gosling's BBC radio 4 broadcast 'Crooning Buffoons: A Sermon on the Evils of Rock and Roll Music' (1982), a rare treat is in store.

3

Working-class youth subcultures

This chapter presents material which examines the class element in working-class youth subcultures in much greater detail than the 'youth culture' approach. Most, but not all of the works referred to adopt a Marxist perspective. This is reflected in the section on terminology below.

The central work discussed is Stuart Hall and Tony Jefferson (eds) *Resistance through Rituals* (1976). Dick Hebdige, a contributor to *Resistance through Rituals*, also wrote *Subculture: The Meaning of Style* (1979). These two publications, taken together, provide a cultural analysis of youth subcultures from the Marxist point of view typical of the Centre for Contemporary Cultural Studies (CCCS) at Birmingham University. There is a considerable body of work analysing aspects of working-class youth subcultures besides these two volumes and I have used this to present certain key features: anti-school subcultures, and leisure, pleasure, and delinquency.

Some of the authors referred to in these sections are very close in perspective to Hall and Jefferson, others much less so. However, I have found that a thematic rather than a 'schools of thought' approach enabled me to present more authentically the feelings and experiences of the subcultural actors. The next section attempts to place analysis of working-class youth subcultures in a broader class and social context. Finally, I compare and contrast the Hall/Jefferson/Hebdige approach with structural and subcultural perspectives on working-class youth.

Terminology and theoretical perspective

Culture and subculture are key terms in this chapter. According to Raymond Williams, culture is the 'relationships between elements in a whole way of life'. E.B. Tylor gave a similar but much fuller definition in 1871: 'Culture ... is that complex whole which includes knowledge, belief, art, morals, law, custom, and any other capabilities and habits acquired by man as a member of society.' E.P. Thompson insists, and Williams agrees, that culture includes relationships reflecting conflict as well as consensus.

A subculture exists when the way of life of a particular group is sufficiently distinctive to give its members a characteristic identity and to differentiate them from the majority or dominant culture. M.M. Gordon (1978) refers to 'social conditions such as class status, ethnic background, regional and urban residence, and religious affiliation' which can provide the basis for the formation of a subculture. No subculture exists entirely independently of the dominant culture, and subcultural analysis largely focuses on the interaction between the two.

Hall and Jefferson use three key concepts in their analysis of postwar youth subcultures: ideology, hegemony, and resistance. They appear to adopt an orthodox Marxist usage of the term ideology. Marx related ideology to class position. The 'true' ideology (consciously held beliefs) of the bourgeoisie represents their interests while those of the working class represent theirs. However, complete identity of consciousness and class ideological interests rarely occurs. In every society there is a dominant class, and its ideology tends to dominate and influence the consciousness of members of other classes. In capitalist society, bourgeois ideology holds this dominating position. The consciousness of working-class people is, therefore, pulled in two directions – towards socialism, their 'true' class ideology – and towards an acceptance of at least some bourgeois ideological values. Hall and Jefferson analyse this 'struggle', in which they consider working-class youth subcultures play a part.

Hall and Jefferson attempt to expand Marx's original presentation of the contest of interests and ideology in capitalist society by using Antonio Gramsci's concept of hegemony. Hegemony is a particular form of power which the ruling class sometimes achieves. It is the power and 'right' of leadership that comes from ideological dominance – from having successfully persuaded large sections of the working class to 'see things' the way the ruling class sees them, i.e. into a state of false consciousness. In more recent writings, Stuart Hall discusses the rise of Thatcherism in these terms. However, in *Resistance through Rituals* he and Jefferson describe a situation of hegemonic domination beginning to emerge in the early postwar years. Already what they refer to as the 'ideology of affluence' was holding sway over large sections of the working class and diverting them from socialism. Whether or not affluence would spread widely or last long did not detract from its ideological appeal, as the popularity of Harold Macmillan's slogan 'You've never had it so good' suggests.

Hall and Jefferson stress that hegemony can be resisted:

'Hegemony, then, is not universal and "given" to the continuing rule of a particular class. It has to be *won*, worked for, reproduced, sustained. Hegemony is, as Gramsci said, a "moving equilibrium", containing "relations of forces favourable or unfavourable to this or that

43

tendency". It is a matter of the nature of the balance struck between contending classes: the compromises made to sustain it; the relations of force; the solutions adopted. Its character and content can only be established by looking at concrete situations, at concrete historical moments. The idea of "permanent class hegemony", or of "permanent incorporation" must be ditched.'

(Hall and Jefferson 1976: 40–1)

Hall and Jefferson argue that working-class subcultural activity contains elements of resistance against ruling-class domination and hegemony. They are quite clear that this resistance is rarely political or consciously ideological. It occurs mainly through certain patterns of behaviour (rituals) and cultural styles. It is also, as the use of the term 'resistance' perhaps indicates, largely defensive in nature. How, then, do Hall and Jefferson and their co-authors interpret the behaviour and style of members of working-class subcultures to establish that 'resistance' is actually taking place? They do so by the use of semiology, and I shall explain what this is in the next section.

In summary, Hall and Jefferson stress that the interaction of culture/subculture involves an active response on the part of subcultural members to the constraints and possibilities of structural location. 'Resistance' is an assertion of identity, of making yourself felt.

Subcultures: rituals, style, and resistance

The contributors to *Resistance through Rituals* attempted to interpret the meaning of mainly working-class youth subcultures in postwar Britain. The theoretical framework of the book is Marxist but the authors' use of semiology immediately established the book as original and challenging. Dick Hebdige, a contributor to the collection, further developed the application of semiology to subcultural analysis in *Subculture: The Meaning of Style* (1979).

Semiology is the study of the meaning(s) of signs. A sign 'stands for' or signifies something else. Thus road traffic signs signify that a given behaviour is required. Signs can change in meaning or mean different things in different contexts (e.g. a clenched fist might signify solidarity or aggression). Crucially, the Birmingham 'school' adopt the view that people may wear or carry signs without being conscious of what they mean by doing so. Thus people may wear sexually provocative clothing without really recognizing the signals they are giving out. The task of the semiologist is to 'decode' or interpret the meanings of signs. The authors of the above books do this by linking signs (displayed through style) with social structure. As Marxists, their main reference points for interpreting signs are social class and the dominant socio-cultural system (the images and ideology of which are conveyed chiefly through the media). Phil Cohen, who was a creative influence on the CCCS in the early 1970s, identified four modes for the generation of subcultural style: dress, music, ritual, and argot (subcultural slang). While not exclusive, these modes provide useful reference categories. The term ritual perhaps needs explanation. It refers to the ordered and repeated expression of a particular collective behaviour – such as chanting or scarf-display at football matches. Uncovering meaning and order in apparently spontaneous and disordered behaviour is very much what the CCCS was about.

Tony Jefferson's article 'Cultural Responses of the Teds: The Defence of Space and Status' is a good example of the Marxist semiology of the CCCS. Jefferson describes the teds as a lower working-class group who felt threatened by immigrants and despised by respectable people generally. They compensated for this both by aggressive/defensive behaviour and by seeking status through style. Somewhat ironically, Jefferson describes their adoption and modification of Savile Row Edwardian suits as their 'one contribution to culture'. He goes on to discuss the bootlace tie worn by many of them. The passage merits consideration as a fairly typical example of the approach under discussion:

'But what "social reality" was their uniform both "expressive of" and "a negotiation with"? Unfortunately there is, as yet, no "grammar" for decoding cultural symbols like dress and what follows is largely speculative. However, if one examines *the context from which the cultural symbol was probably extracted* – one possible way of formulating one aspect of such a grammar – then the adoption of, for example, the bootlace tie, begins to acquire social meaning. Probably picked up from the many American Western films viewed during this period where it was worn, most prevalently as I remember them, by the slick city gambler whose social status was, grudgingly, high because of his ability to live *by his wits* and *outside* the traditional working-class *mores* of society (which were basically rural and hardworking as opposed to urban and hedonistic), then I believe its symbolic cultural meaning for the Teds becomes explicable as both expression of their *social reality* (basically outsiders and forced to live by their wits) and their *social "aspirations"* (basically an attempt to gain high, albeit grudging, status for an ability to live smartly, hedonistically and by their wits in an urban setting).'

(Jefferson in Hall and Jefferson 1976: 86)

Dick Hebdige's analysis of the mods presents them as conspicuous consumers who manage to transform the commodities they buy. Thus the scooter, normally an 'ultra-respectable means of transport' became 'a weapon and symbol of solidarity' when ridden in menacing pack formation. If the mods toyed with fantasies of wealth, higher status, and even refinement, the skinheads dealt more in the symbolism of traditional working-class community and masculinity. In a seminal article written as early as 1972, Phil Cohen explained their aggressive, anti-immigrant, 'territorially' defensive behaviour in the context of the decline of East End working-class communities. 'In reality', they could not reconstruct what was being lost but, in John Clarke's phrase, they performed a 'magical recovery of community' by their behaviour. In one of the most brilliant (because once stated, quite obvious) Marxist-inspired semiological interpretations, Cohen decodes their 'uniform' – Doc Marten boots, braces, collarless shirts, and cropped hair – as a dramatized, exaggerated version of traditional, male, working-class attire.

In *Subculture: The Meaning of Style*, Dick Hebdige continues the history of subcultures through 'glam and glitter rock' to punk. Hebdige suggests that David Bowie appealed to a 'mass youth' audience with a message of fantasy and escape. Strictly, then, 'glam rock' was not a subcultural style but more closely embedded in the forces of 'mass' youth culture discussed in Chapter 2. Despite his socially and politically uncommitted and ambiguous posture, Bowie did raise one issue sharply – that of the nature of sexual identity. His sheer ingenuity and skill in dramatic experiment make it difficult to dismiss him as a mere 'dupe of the system'.

Hebdige sees punk as an attempt to expose the extravagance and remoteness of 'glam rock' while still using some of its stylistic techniques. Punk was in part a response to rising youth unemployment. Punks dramatized the plight of working-class youth by wearing cheap, patched-together clothes, repulsively 'glammed up'. As Hebdige says, punk carried 'the political bite, so obviously missing in most contemporary white music'. But it was a sharp explosion of anarchy, a violent 'capitulation to alienation' rather than rational politics that characterized punk. Somewhat controversially, Hebdige argues that punk adopted the values of 'anarchy', 'surrender', and 'decline' from black reggae music.

Incorporating subcultures: commerce and the media

The deviant elements in subcultures offend the dominant order and attempts are made to incorporate them into 'society'. Hebdige describes two characteristic forms of this process of takeover or incorporation.

'1 the conversion of subcultural signs (dress, music, etc.) into mass-produced objects (i.e. the commodity form);
2 the labelling and redefinition of deviant behaviour by

dominant groups – the police, the media, the judiciary (i.e. the ideological form).'   (Hebdige 1979: 94)

As Hebdige says, the commodity form of incorporation 'has been comprehensively handled by both journalists and academics'. As we saw in Chapter 2, capitalist enterprise is always keen to package and market profitable items of subcultural creativity. Hebdige observes that 'Punk clothing and insignia could be bought mail-order by the summer of 1977, and in September of that year *Cosmopolitan* ran a review of Zandra Rhodes's latest collection of couture follies which consisted entirely of variations on the punk theme.' I can add from my own recollection that punk regalia was certainly in *Vogue* magazine. Digressing slightly, perhaps the most paradoxical commodity incorporation of 'anti-system' behaviour was the use of the romantic face of the deadly serious revolutionary, Che Guevara, on millions of mass-produced tee-shirts and wall-mirrors ('Che lives'??).

Hebdige suggests two 'basic strategies' of the ideological form of incorporation. 'First, the other can be trivialized, naturalized, domesticated. Here, the difference is simply denied ("Otherness is reduced to sameness"). Alternatively, the Other can be transformed into meaningless exotica, a "pure object, a spectacle, a clown" (Barthes 1972).' Hebdige found 'an equal number of articles' incorporating punk on the basis of either its ordinariness or its triviality.

It seems to me that Hebdige's analysis fully corresponds with the established thinking of Hall on media/subcultural interaction. Yet Trowler and Riley (1984: 153) suggest that Hebdige uses the concept of incorporation as follows: 'The .... point Hebdige makes in qualifying the CCCS position is that the youth subcultures are not allowed independence by the capitalist world in which they exist.' In fact, appreciation of this point is a central theoretical feature of *Resistance through Rituals*.

In comment, the rise and fall of subcultures suggests that commerce and the media do successfully incorporate them.

Equally, new or 'old' but revitalized subcultural forms rise up. Gosling refers to subcultural noise as 'a roar of working-class discontent'. Whether there remains the energy in that roar to generate more subcultural activity remains to be seen. If not, we must look to create new forms. Otherwise 'the system' itself will surely provide them for us.

Any review of the above works must recognize their original and imaginative contribution to the tradition of Marxist socio-cultural analysis. Taken as a collective enterprise, they achieve a synthesis of structural and cultural analysis which is sensitive to dynamic and historical factors. In addition to structures and cultures, the authors recognize the need to present individual biographies. They accept that they can only do this to a limited extent, but their analytical framework has the potential for a fuller expression of personal voice and life history. This is demonstrated in the work of Paul Willis, formerly a research fellow at the CCCS, whose work we examine in the next section.

A first question about *Resistance through Rituals* and *Subculture: The Meaning of Style* can usefully focus on the issue of interpretation. It can be argued that the element of 'resistance' in working-class youth subcultures is over-represented. In fairness, Hall and Jefferson point out that sub-cultural resistance is not political, nor is it an adequate 'solution' to the problems faced by working-class youth. They also recognize that: 'The energies and aspirations expressed within subcultures can easily be diverted into conventional channels of consumer or status concern.' So what, then, is the nature and scope of this resistance? Their claim is that it is a resistance through 'style' or 'ritual'. The lads' 'spectacular', 'magical' behaviour rarely becomes an overt challenge to the dominant ideology or hegemony, but Hall and Jefferson do show that there is a limited class-based 'ideological dimension' both to the style and focal concerns of the subcultural factors, i.e. ideological in their involvement with working-class interests. They attempt to 'win space' just as their parents win space in their traditional cultural activities. They create a certain margin of collective freedom and expression. However, 'resistance' is perhaps not the best descriptive term for this process. The word 'negotiation', sometimes used by Hall and Jefferson, seems a more neutral and precise base term. Subcultural negotiation can involve adjustment as well as resistance to dominant structures. But very often subcultural activities seem to be less categorizable than either term accommodates. Stanley Cohen's comment that it is more complicated, contradictory, and ambiguous than Hall and Jefferson suggest is worth considering. For instance, to interpret skinhead activities as 'resistance' rather than, say, the product of angry frustration is, finally, highly subjective. Their victims could be fairly random but included a large proportion of Asians. Hall and Jefferson do not interpret this violence in political terms, but it seems to reflect the fascist rather than traditionally stronger socialist strain in East End working-class behaviour. In such cases – indeed, in any case – there is nothing 'magical' about being beaten up by a skinhead.

In arguably overplaying the term 'resistance' and in trying to shape their analysis to structural conflict, Hall and Jefferson overall give too romantic and simplified a picture of working-class youth subcultures. They themselves are not only more interested in class issues than the subcultural actors but, after all, perceive them quite differently. We would turn the tables on Hall and Jefferson and 'decode' their motives – perhaps they are projecting their own fantasies of resistance onto the 'lads'. Another interpretation – and interpretations do differ – might find the lads much more happily involved in the objects of American-inspired 'mass' culture and less 'resistant' to the system, even symbolically, than Hall and Jefferson imagine. If Hall and Jefferson's class-based analysis of resistance leads them into over-simplification, their use of semiology may result in false 'discovery' by faulty 'decoding'.

A second observation about the above work is that it deals only partially with certain groups: 'ordinary' or conformist youth; girls; and parents. Hall and Jefferson are entitled to examine youth subcultures rather than the lives of the majority of young people who do not 'join' them. However, to maintain a fuller perspective it is important to remember the relative conformity of most teenagers (albeit that they conform within different class, ethnic, regional, and other contexts). The absence of girls in most accounts of working-class subcultures is noted by Angela McRobbie and Jenny Garber in 'Girls and Subcultures' in *Resistance through Rituals*. The book as a whole bears out their point, though their own article is an excellent beginning to establishing a body of work in this area (see pp. 59–60). The absence of data about parents of participants in working-class youth subcultures is surprising. One way of establishing their thesis that there is substantial continuity between generations of working-class people would have been for Hall and Jefferson to produce comparative information on the generations about values, attitudes, and beliefs. Presumably, however, this would have involved a sizeable social survey.

Third, it is arguable that in concentrating on the resistance, as they saw it, of a relatively small section of working-class youth, Hall and Jefferson may have been misled about the broader and longer-term trends affecting not only working-class youth but the working class as a whole. Had they looked at 'respectable' and upwardly mobile working-class youths they may have had to conclude that the tendency to accommodate to certain aspects of 'the system' among the working class was deeper and less easily reversible than they hoped. Perhaps this point can be made more clearly by reference to an earlier study of working-class youth by Peter Willmott (1966). Willmott's *Adolescent Boys of East London* divides the boys into three groups: the rebel, the 'typical' working-class boy ('typical' is my term), and the middle-class boy. The rebel is the type of 'lad' Hall and Jefferson focus on and is the main subject of this chapter. The working-class boy goes to school with no great enthusiasm, spends money as freely as he can, and looks forward to going to work. The middle-class boy is not our concern here. However, I would argue that a third category of working-class boy can usefully be added to Willmott's two.

This is the working-class boy who intends to 'make good', to achieve upward social mobility. There is much circumstantial data to substantiate the existence of such a type in considerable numbers in the postwar period, though there may have been fewer in such a relatively 'solid' working-class area as East London. Halsey, Heath, and Ridge's *Origins and Destinations* (1980) shows that about a third of the working class were upwardly mobile during much of the postwar period (though it was probably much less in the 1970s and 1980s, which are outside their survey). It would seem likely, then, that an upwardly mobile working-class type existed widely.

In any case, the diversity of working-class youth is probably much greater than Hall and Jefferson consider. It seems safe to state that the unrebellious, 'typical' working-class boy and the upwardly oriented type make up the overwhelming majority. Many adult males, once in these categories, have become relatively affluent and a significant number, probably a majority, do not vote Labour. Though apparently aware of the existence of these groups and of the socio-economic trends that formed their attitudes, Hall and Jefferson give them scant attention. Instead they concentrate on what may be the fading 'resistance' of a few. That is their privilege but, from their own Marxist point of view, it may also be 'fiddling while Rome burns'. A fuller analysis of youth might have given them a clearer insight into broader changes in working-class opinion.

Activities

1 Select one youth subculture. To what extent did its members 'resist' through rituals and what were they resisting? (You can illustrate your points from the words of songs, magazines, etc.)
2 Referring to the quotation from Tony Jefferson and the relevant text, how convincing do you find his interpretation of the 'teds' and, especially, his 'decoding' of their style?

Aspects of working-class youth subcultures: anti-school subcultures, leisure, pleasure, and delinquency

The purpose of this section is to overview certain aspects of working-class youth subcultures. I shall explore the following themes within the areas of behaviour indicated in the title: poor communication and conflict with authority; 'having fun'; a preference for practice over theory; masculinity among boys and femininity/domesticity among girls; territoriality; and a tendency to create informal structures which can be controlled, and to reject or avoid formal ones which cannot. Part of Hall's and Jefferson's purpose is precisely to point out these characteristics of working-class youth and their continuity with those of working-class adults. However, not all working-class youth participate in the 'spectacular' subcultures. It helps to locate these class characteristics in the fundamental processes that structure their lives and within which they 'negotiate' their life styles. Several of the authors cited below either worked at the Centre for Contemporary Cultural Studies in Birmingham or contributed to *Resistance through Rituals*. They include Paul Willis, Paul Corrigan, Angela McRobbie, and Phil Cohen. The quality of the other contributions shows, however, that the Centre has no monopoly on youth subcultural analysis in Britain.

Although still mainly concerned with lower working-class male subculture, this section is slightly broader in scope than the previous one. It deals, at least in passing, with the 'respectable' as well as the 'rough', the 'conformist' as well as the 'nonconformist', the 'lobes' as well as the 'lads'.

Anti-school subcultures

An anti-school subculture is a group of young people who opt out of the academic goals of the educational system and find their main expression in pleasure-seeking leisure activities. Its members tend either actively or passively to oppose the school hierarchy and smooth functioning of the school. The majority of anti-school subcultures are working class, and they have

53

been found to arise in grammar, secondary modern, and comprehensive schools. In this section we will attempt to find out why.

The role of the school   Two studies carried out in the 1960s provide a useful starting point for analysis: David Hargreaves's case-study, *Social Relations in a Secondary School* (1967) established that the policy of streaming pursued in the school was a factor in contributing to the formation of an anti-school subculture among lower stream boys. In his study *Hightown Grammar* (1970), Colin Lacey found the same process at work. He introduced two terms, differentiation and polarization, which describe two aspects of what occurs: one initiated by teachers, the other by pupils:

'By *differentiation* I mean the separation and ranking of studentsaccording to a multiple set of criteria which makes up the normative, academically oriented, value system of the grammar school. Differentiation is defined here as being largely carried out by teachers in the course of their normal duties.

Polarization, on the other hand, takes place within the student body partly as a result of differentiation, but influenced by external factors and with an autonomy of its own. It is a process of subculture formation in which the school-dominated, normative culture is opposed by an alternative culture.'   (Lacey 1970: 57)

Stephen Ball's *Beachside Comprehensive: A Case-study of Secondary Schooling* (1981) presents, in his own words, 'a model essentially similar to those identified by Hargreaves and Lacey': a pro-school band 1 and anti-school bands 2 and 3. However, Ball sees the Hargreaves-Lacey model as too simple and he develops it further. He classifies the pro-school group into those who support the formal school system out of moral conviction (supportive) and those who simply use it for their own ends to obtain qualifications (manipulative). He classifies the anti-school group into those who ignore the school's formal structure without resorting to active opposition

54

(passive) and those who are overtly alienated from the goals and authority of the school (rejecting). All three observers note that it is teachers who mediate the process of class polarization by filtering or differentiating pupils through their own middle-class value system. Not surprisingly, they observe that the process of polarization tends to increase from the second year to the fourth and fifth as pupils become committed to particular forms of adaptation and identity, and the decisive juncture of public examinations approaches.

'Lads and lobes' The above observers' description of polarization in three schools can be checked against interview data with pupils themselves. Ball, in particular, did this. Two further studies are rich in detail about pupils' own experiences of school: Paul Willis's Learning to Labour: How Working-class Kids Get Working-class Jobs (1977) and Paul Corrigan's Schooling the Smash Street Kids (1979). As their titles indicate, these works concentrate mainly on the overtly anti-school group who Ball refers to as rejecting and who in Willis's study refer to themselves as 'the lads'. Willis carried out one main, intensive case-study of twelve non-academic working-class lads at the same school, and five comparative studies of other groups of male pupils. Corrigan's study is about 'working-class boys at school and their delinquent behaviour'. He mixed freely with lads at two schools and obtained questionnaire and interview data from forty-eight at one school and question-naire data only from forty-five at the other.

We now examine the lads' responses. First, the lack of communication and depth of conflict between the boys and school authorities is indicated by the following extract from an interview by Corrigan:

'Question Do you think teachers understand boys?
Edward Well, like the way the boys act, the teachers don't understand 'cos some of the teachers are old, and in any case they are different from us, and we're young and have got our own ways. They don't know what it's like to be young and live on this estate.

Question   In the questionnaire you said that you thought that teachers were 'big-heads'.
Edward   Well, some are because they think, ah, they're a teacher and they think that they can rule you in school and tell you what to do and where to go and all that.
Question   Do many of the boys not like this?
Edward   Aye, hordes of them don't, because the teachers are always picking on them and that.
Question   Are you going to stay on at all?
Edward   No, I'm leaving this summer.'

(Corrigan 1979: 54)

Joey, one of the lads in Willis's main case-study, also described what he experiences as a situation of naked power-conflict with authority:

'They're able to punish us. They're bigger than us, they stand for a bigger establishment than we do, like, we're just little and they stand for bigger things, and you try to get your own back. It's, uh, resenting authority I suppose.'

(Willis 1977: 11)

A major interest of the lads is 'having fun' or, to use the jargon, pursuing short-term hedonism (pleasure). School is not the obvious place in which to find fun, but the lads do the best they can. Two major objects of fun present themselves in schools: teachers and hard-working pupils whom the lads call 'lobes' and who might correspond to Ball's pro-school supportive and manipulative subgroups. In looking for fun and often finding it in 'taking the mick' out of authority, the lads are merely acting inside school as they do in their own street and neighbourhood environment. They continue to pursue what middle-class pupils might consider to be leisure values within the school context. This is clear in the following extract from an interview by Corrigan:

'*Question*   Lots of boys … carrying on. What does it mean?
Tony   Well, it means that we do what we do outside class. Talk, shout, eat, muck about. Just what we always do.

Question   What do teachers do?

Tony   They don't like it. But what can they do? They can't rule you, can they?'   (Corrigan 1979: 55)

Even 'in fun' the conflict with authority is apparent. The occasions of truce seem to occur when the lads can 'have a laff' *with* rather than *against* a teacher, or when a teacher is sufficiently respected to command attention (paradoxically, this is usually when a teacher wields effective authority).

Willis and Corrigan particularly examine the relationship between the lads' experience of school including, usually, examination failure, and their future (or lack of it) in the world of work. As we have seen, the 'future' is not a strong preoccupation of the lads. By contrast, a group of conformist boys interviewed by Willis do see an obvious relationship between school and work, with qualifications providing the link. They also take an interest in career films and interviews.

According to Corrigan, the lads 'basically reject the idea of qualifications'. This is logical given that they have already rejected the apparent means of obtaining them – conformity to school norms – and have usually been rejected as 'good examination material' by teachers. They feel that qualifications merely represent useless theoretical knowledge and do not relate to the reality of the physical work traditionally valued by the working class. This attitude underlies the response of Spike, one of the lads, to Paul Willis's question:

'*Paul Willis*   What is it that you think you've got that the ear'oles haven't?

Spike   Guts, determination, not guts, cheek as well ... we know more about life than they do. They might know a bit more about maths and science which isn't important.'

(Willis 1977: 95)

In fact, the lads do get jobs, or rather they did in the mid-1970s, the period of Willis's and Corrigan's research. Willis gives some examples: 'Tyre fitting, carpet laying, trainee machinists in a furniture factory, plumbers' and bricklayers' mate, upholstering in a car-seat firm, bar loading in a chromium plate factory, painting and decorating.' They got these jobs, not by flourishing qualifications, but by reading the situations vacant column in the local newspaper and by checking workplaces for vacancies. Mostly, they expected jobs to be boring, like school, but a job paid money and it was always possible to leave. At least a job was real work and offered a basic physical satisfaction and sometimes demanded practical skill, unlike school.

Some comments on the above work are appropriate. First, it substantially contributes to our understanding of how the educational system (and the typical role of the teacher within it) helps to reproduce and confirm class cultural differences and fails to bring about full equality of opportunity, despite some individual successes by working-class children.

Second, we must be as clear as the current state of research allows on the precise role of the educational system in contributing to the creation of anti-school subcultures. Streaming or banding is only one factor and not the decisive one. Ball, for instance, found polarization taking place *within* as well as *between* bands, as well as a number of pupils who did not adhere clearly to either pro- or anti-school values. Significantly, Willis found an anti-school group and a pro-school group within one *mixed-ability* class. Perhaps the deeper cause of polarization within the educational system are the public examinations, which broadly reflect middle-class academic values and are mainly implemented by middle-class people (teachers). Despite recent changes, the practical activities respected by the lads are rarely given equal facilities and status with academic ones in the British educational system. The fundamental cause of polarization, however, lies in the class nature of British society itself which the educational system helps to reproduce (see pp. 61–3).

A third comment is that, taken as a whole, the body of work under discussion is sexist. Four of the researchers studied only male anti-school subcultures. Ball's work was based on a mixed-sex comprehensive and, while his presentation gives a balanced coverage of both sexes, he says relatively little about

58

the role of girls, individually or collectively, in anti-school subcultures.

Girls Like the lads, the girls 'learn to labour' by a dual process of institutional elimination and self-elimination from alternative possibilities. They are eliminated from educational and many forms of career success by being labelled academic failures, and they eliminate themselves by opting for the non-academic activities they prefer to school work. This section is about how they express their experience of this complex process, and is based on Angela McRobbie's article 'Working-class Girls and the Culture of Femininity'. McRobbie studied fifty-six working-class girls aged between fourteen and sixteen who lived on the same council estate, attended the same school, and frequented Mill Lane youth club. Her research techniques included 'participant observation, taped and untaped interviews, questionnaires, informal discussions, and diary-keeping'.

The girls are subject to two forms of subordination: class and gender. In other words, they are subordinated to capitalism and patriarchy (a male-dominant system of gender relations). Thus their destination as adults is to do low-status, unpaid work – housework – much of which is concerned with maintaining the male labour force and children. The jobs they do take up, outside of domestic work, are generally of low pay and status. Typically they are short term, part time, or both.

The girls do not consider that the school, as a formal institution, is very relevant to their future domestic role or, still less, to the immediate matter of 'getting a man'. Like the lads, they develop an anti-school subculture which is largely gender based. It is similarly anti-authoritarian or, as McRobbie refers to it, 'oppositional'. Like the anti-school subculture of the lads it takes the major forms of 'playing up' teachers and ridiculing middle-class and/or hard-working pupils (in their case, mainly girls). The second point is illustrated by the following comment by one of the girls, Maggie, who criticizes the 'swots' or 'snobs' for academic orientation and sexual naïvety:

> 'They all think they're brainy but they're not. I mean Karen and me, we do no work but if we wanted to we could be top of the class. We're just interested in other things. They just want to be top, they're not ... they don't like boys or nothing.'

The 'other things' the girls are interested in indicate the positive, pleasure-seeking side of their behaviour. In their chosen areas, they achieve 'successes' despite, and in opposition to, the school, not because of it. As McRobbie puts it, their achievements 'hinged on their ability to work the system and to transform the school into the sphere, *par excellence*, for developing their social life, fancying boys, learning the latest dance, having a smoke together in the lavatories and playing up the teachers'.

Like Willis and Corrigan, McRobbie is interested in how, as adults, her group end up doing the work they do. The answer is the same. The 'kids' reject an institution which they experience as rejecting them. Here is Maggie again: 'They don't care, nobody in this school cares, the head said to me last week she just wants us to leave, they treat you like you was dirt.' Maggie's remark is not presented as objective or necessarily typical, but it will have a familiar ring to many teachers and pupils in secondary schools, particularly those with a large working-class intake. McRobbie herself is certainly not a structural determinist in the sense of believing that schools inevitably 'churn out' working-class failures and middle-class successes. She is aware that pupils do cross the cultural and academic divide. She particularly points out that female teachers who may have struggled hard for their job themselves can be particularly effective in helping girls, including working-class girls, to make academic and career decisions which reflect other ambitions than simply those of traditional, working-class girls. But most of them end up in domestic work and/or as a reserve pool of cheap and pliable labour.

60

Anti-school subcultures, class, and society Sociologists have become more dubious about the capacity of the educational system to change society and increasingly aware of its role in reproducing society as it is. In the 1960s and 1970s there was much optimism, especially in the Labour Party, that the comprehensive system could be used as an instrument to compensate for the effect of class inequalities and to help bring about equality of opportunity. The comprehensive system may yet play a role in these respects but the evidence of its capacity to do so is ambiguous. It seems that there is not much difference between the results obtained under the tripartite system (grammar, secondary modern, and technical schools) and the comprehensive system when social class is held constant. There is also a considerable body of research, in addition to that reviewed in this chapter, which suggests that comprehensive schools, as well as other types of secondary schools, contribute to the reproduction of class cultural differences. These cultural differences lead directly to material and status inequalities in occupational selection. The reproduction of social class by the educational system is not total. A significant number of working-class 'kids' do obtain above-average examination results and get 'middle-class' jobs, just as a significant number of middle-class 'kids' do not. However, this is not the general picture and the trend is as we have described it.

The fundamental reason why class inequality is reproduced from generation to generation must be sought in the nature of capitalist society itself. Capitalism requires a working class. The less skilled section of the working class is recruited largely from academic 'failures', although some have low-level vocational qualifications. The more skilled may have served apprenticeships or obtained other work-related qualifications, but many will also have experienced the stigma of academic failure. This is inevitable given that the educational system reserves its most meaningful qualification – an 'O' level pass or above – for about 20 per cent per subject of a given school year. Until the recent high levels of unemployment, the lads 'fitted in' at the lower end of the occupational hierarchy, though some might have 'made it' to the level of skilled worker or even set up in small businesses.

French Marxists Althusser and Bourdieu, American Marxist Harry Braverman, and British Marxist Paul Willis, argue that the experience of educational failure in capitalist society not only forces working-class pupils to take working-class jobs but actually prepares them to do so, particularly those who take up lower level jobs. This is because the values and attitudes of the anti-school subculture correspond with those of lower working-class men. The following extract from Willis explains how the lads experience this correspondence:

'The located "lads" culture, as part of the general class culture, supplies a set of "unofficial" criteria by which to judge generally *what kind* of working situation is going to be most relevant to the individual. It has to be work where he can be open about his desires, his sexual feelings, his liking for "booze" and his aim to "skive off" as much as is reasonably possible. It has to be a place where people can be trusted and will not "creep off" to tell the boss about "foreigners" or "nicking stuff" – in effect where there are the fewest "ear'oles". Indeed, it would have to be work where there was a boss, a "them and us" situation, which always carried with it the danger of treacherous inter-mediaries. The future work situation has to have an essentially masculine ethos. It has to be a place where people are not "cissies" and can "handle themselves", where "pen-pushing" is looked down on in favour of really "doing things". It has to be a situation where you can speak up for yourself, and where you would not be expected to be subservient. The principal visible criterion is that the particular job must pay good money quickly and offer the possibility of "fiddles" and "perks" to support already acquired smoking and drinking habits and to nourish the sense of being "on the inside track", of knowing "how things really work". Work has to be a place, basically, where people are "alright" and with whom a general cultural identity can be shared.'

(Willis 1977: 96)

As Willis explores elsewhere in his book, masculinity, toughness, loyalty, rough humour, underlying and often ingeniously pursued anti-authoritarianism, and enjoyment of basic pleasures are also the values of adult working men. The lads 'escape' the boring conformity demanded by school but they are 'caught' by their own conformity to class norms, and thus they 'learn to labour'.

Angela McRobbie makes the same point about her sample of working-class girls, with the difference that the class norms they identify with are family based and female specific. For most of them jobs are only of secondary and often temporary interest. They consider that their labour is to care for men and children, and whether they enjoy it or not they are trapped within it:

'Marriage, family life, fashion and beauty all contribute massively to this feminine anti-school culture and, in doing so, nicely illustrate the contradictions inherent in so-called oppositional activities. Are the girls in the end not simply doing exactly what is required of them – and if this *is* the case, then could it not be convincingly argued that it is their own culture which itself is the most effective agent of social control for girls, pushing them into compliance with that role which a whole range of institutions in capitalist society also, but less effectively, directs them towards? At the same time, the girls are expressing a class relation, in albeit traditionally feminine terms. As one girl, "Wendy", put it:

"We don't need the teachers to tell us. But we like to have a good time. There's plenty of time to study when you're older. Me dad would like me to study more. He wants me to get a good job. He's a shop steward and he's always telling me about his union and that. Getting me to read the papers. But I'm not interested now. I like to go out every night with Christine. We like to have a good time at school. Play up the teachers, talk about boys."'

(McRobbie 1978a: 104)

63

Leisure, pleasure, and delinquency in working-class youth subcultures

Until recently, sociologists have tended to think of leisure primarily in terms of how it is influenced by the type of work a person does. Thus Stanley Parker (1971) categorized much working-class leisure activity as oppositional to work, particularly where work is repetitive, restrictive, and unfulfilling. Leisure provides time to relax and recuperate, compensating for the drudgery of work. Obviously, such a model is of limited usefulness in understanding the leisure activities of working-class youths, most of whom are still at school. In any case, other models of analysing leisure which consider more fully major variables such as gender, age, and class culture in influencing leisure patterns are now being developed. Paul Corrigan sees continuities (similarities) in the values and behaviour of the lads both in and out of school. School and work impose more restrictions than 'free time', but the lads behave true to type in most situations. The same perspective underlies David Robins and Phil Cohen's analysis of a group of urban, working-class youth, *Knuckle Sandwich: Growing Up in the Working-class City* (1979).

Wherever we analyse the leisure activity of the lads, we find similarities in their behaviour: on the streets, on the football terraces, 'knocking around' a youth club, or at a dance-hall. At an obvious level what they are after is fun. Sometimes, giving the appearance of 'doing nothing', 'hanging about', they are often poised to create 'a bit of excitement' or do something 'for a laugh'. On occasions, this can result in 'accidents' to objects like windows or milk bottles, and people like policemen or teachers. Even in their more laid-back moments, the lads are creatively involved in 'taking the piss' out of each other.

In adopting the lads' own description of much of their leisure activity as 'having fun', we should be careful not to underestimate them. As Corrigan (1979: 117) points out, the lads seek to construct and control their own activities, and avoid or oppose those who try to take this freedom away from them: 'It is essential for the boys to be allowed to create their own *structure* of activity. This is true in the fields of playing and watching sport, as well as music.'

We have already seen the antagonistic attitude of the lads to school authority. When they attend youth clubs, they tend to avoid formal activities organized by 'youth leaders'. The streets and open ground are among their preferred areas of activity and football the game they play most often. It seems to me that the (self) control and expression the lads seek in their leisure activities is a compensation for the pressure to conform at school (though even there they 'battle' for their own way). The following passage from Robins and Cohen describes the difference between the lads' 'self-constructed' game of football and that imposed by keen school coaches:

'Despite the sign NO BALL GAMES, every evening improvised games of football would be played out on the courtyards and bare patches of grass around the Monmouth and Deny. Kids of all ages, shapes, and sizes would take part in these, often in platform heels, smart jackets or tight trousers. Rules, playing area, goals, team numbers were all negotiable. What was harder to negotiate was the co-operation of the tenants. The broken windows, noise, and disturbance caused by these games were amongst the biggest source of complaints that the Tenants' Association Committee was called upon to deal with. Invariably, such matches would end in heated confrontations with angry tenants and the police being called.

Such casual disruptive exertions of physical energy tended to be seen by school coaches and club men such as Jock as little more than self-generating rituals practised by the kids as they are supposed to have done since time immemorial. Part of the local scenery. Quite different from the mini-professional training, coaching, and adult-controlled sporting discipline as practised in club and school soccer. As one coach put it: "There's very little competitiveness, very little possessiveness, on or off the ball, when they play in the street. They just get pleasure from making the ball move from one to another in a certain way, or just mucking about or showing off. But without any real energy put into it. In the youth club there's a lot more real fire goes into it ... mind you, if I left them in the gym by themselves, if I wasn't there to watch them, they'd play like that." Indeed, exactly the same kids would play these two styles out.'

(Robins and Cohen 1979: 128–29)

The activities of male working-class youth frequently have a collective or group orientation, and a concern for territory. These two aspects often occur together, giving an almost tribal quality to the lads' behaviour, notably when gang warfare occurs. Their territoriality is not focused primarily on the possession of a precise physical area but is more a matter of psychological assertion and masculinity. Robins and Cohen make the point well:

'What we refer to as "territoriality" is a symbolic process of magically appropriating, owning, and controlling the material environment in which you live, but which in real, economic and political terms is owned and controlled by "outsiders" – in our society, by private landlords or the state. It applies, therefore, almost exclusively to working-class areas. And it has to be understood in class terms.'

(Robins and Cohen 1979: 73)

Football matches provide a highly appropriate context for young working-class males to adopt territorially aggressive/defensive postures. They do so by performing 'tribal' rituals (chants, songs, and, sometimes, primitive jigs) and by adopting ceremonial styles (team scarves and caps, etc.). According to Marsh, Rosser, and Harré (1978), the lads are much more organized than they might appear superficially. He argues that most football 'ends', 'sheds' or 'kops' divide into at least three subgroups. Marsh makes the following divisions of the popular terraces at Oxford United where he did a special study:

		Pitch
Novices		10 or 11 year olds
Town Boys		19 to 25 year olds
Rowdies	1 Nutters	15+ year olds
	2 Hooligans	
	3 Hardcases	

The young novices divide their attention between the game and admiring the activities of the rowdies at the back. The town boys, usually tough young men, have the authority and status of those who have already proved themselves. The rowdies form what Marsh refers to as the 'core membership of the terrace culture'. The rowdies have a number of specialized roles or 'career' choices open to them. A hardcase or aggro leader is the highest status role within the rowdies. He is a fighter, the first in and last out of clashes with rival fans. Nutters build their reputation on being willing to do 'crazy' or 'mad' things. Unlike the hardcases, nutters take unnecessary risks and may inflict excessive damage. They force the rest of the rowdies to recognize that there are 'limits' and 'rules', and other members of the group often restrain the nutters' worst excesses. Hooligans are jesters: their actions are aimed at enraging or making fools of people rather than damaging them.

Most sociological observers see powerfully positive and negative sides to the lads' behaviour. First, the positive side. The lads create an often entertaining and expressive way of life which reflects much of the parent working-class culture. The story of the 'dads of the lads' would be another but culturally similar one. Second, the negative side. The lads' culture is laced with aggression and is sometimes violent. Some of this aggression seems to be caused by the frustrations and limitations of their lives. Working-class lads may seldom be consciously angry at 'society', but many seem to simmer with a hidden sense of resentment and injury, which surfaces frequently in their strikes against authority. This complex of feelings approximates to what sociologists refer to as alienation. One of the fans interviewed by Marsh puts it his own way:

'I'm afraid there's got to be some sort of outlet. You see, say in this area. When you leave school and you've got no qualifications, you've got a choice of two jobs: either become a labourer or down't pit. Now it doesn't leave a lot to the week either race dogs or fly pigeons. You're really limited. I think, council have banned pigeons in't back yard and say they banned goats and you've got to find some sort of expression, so violence has become an expression.

It's society innit, you know, if they didn't do it in football ground, you'd do it in pubs, you know, do it .... It's just pride ... pride ... street corners and all that, you know. It's ... in actual fact it's doing society a favour, it's keeping 'em away, keepin' 'em at football grounds and you've got plenty of police on hand an' that .... It is society a lot of it, you know, it's down to society.'

(Marsh, Rosser, and Harré 1978: 80–1)

Working-class youthful delinquency is partly presented as an 'overspill' of pleasure-seeking activity in the above class-based perspective. Some of the behaviour of the young football supporters illustrates this nicely. For instance, damaging property and baiting authority is often 'part of the occasion', bringing no advantage except a degree of status among peers and the release of feeling. This, of course, is not a full and adequate analysis of working-class youth delinquency, much of which is economically motivated. However, it usefully employs the concepts of class and youth to explain behaviour often seen by outsiders as merely senseless.

British and American subcultural theory reviews: the interactionist contribution

Stanley Cohen, who has a somewhat uneasy critical relationship with the CCCS, takes the view that in certain ways their work is less distinctive and innovatory than has sometimes been suggested (Cohen 1979). In particular, he argues that commentators other than the CCCS have had a full appreciation of the role of structural constraints in contributing to the formation of subcultures. Analysis of the relevance of class factors is not unusual, either, and Cohen recommends David Downes's work of the 1960s as illustrative of both points.

Here, however, I shall briefly review some examples of American subcultural theory with Cohen's viewpoint in mind. Cohen also accepts, along with the CCCS, the importance of presenting biographical experience in subcultural analysis and I shall also consider this aspect, finally returning to Cohen's own work.

Robert Merton (1938) is the theoretical 'big daddy' of American subcultural theorists, although his own emphasis was on the consensual value system and legitimate opportunity structure of society. He regarded delinquency as a type of nonconformity which was the product of being shut out of the legitimate opportunity structure. Following on from Merton, Albert Cohen (1955) described lower working-class youth delinquency in terms of 'the mechanism of "reaction formation"'. He states that '(T)he hallmark of the delinquent subculture is the explicit and wholesale repudiation of middle-class standards and the adoption of their very antithesis.' Delinquents savour their status and possessions all the more because they obtain them by opposite means to middle-class America. Cloward and Ohlin (1961) also see lower working-class delinquency as an attempt to solve the problem of a closed legitimate opportunity structure, but describe three types of illegitimate opportunity/structures and related deviant subcultures: criminal, conflict (a reaction into violence due to the frustration of feeling both in the legitimate and criminal opportunity structures), and drug (retreatist).

The above body of theory is of a piece in stressing the role of central values and the legitimate opportunity structure in forming subcultural reaction. Walter Miller (1958) is distinctive in that he argues that lower-class boys tend to have certain *focal* concerns which differentiate them from middle-class boys: these centre on the areas of trouble, toughness, smartness (to 'con' or 'be conned'), excitement, fate (lucky or unlucky), and autonomy (freedom or constraint). Miller works from within the subculture outwards, rather than from the central value system to the subculture.

69

With differing degrees of emphasis, both the 'central value system' and 'lower class' values are employed in explaining subcultural formation in the above works. It is, perhaps, not possible to say whether American or British subcultural theories contain more biographical data. Certainly there is no shortage of individual anecdote and reference to life-history in the American literature. The outstanding example is William Foot Whyte's *Street Corner Society* (1955; first published 1943) which, incidentally, discovered 'rules' and 'order' within apparent subcultural disorder long before Marsh, Rosser, and Harré (1978).

How original and different, then, does the CCCS work look when compared to the above? Both attempt to explain the dynamic relationship between structure and subculture, but with different terminology and interpretation. What the American subcultural theorists see as the adaptive interplay of the (central) social system and lower-class culture, the British Marxists see as a dialectic between the dominant (capitalist) system and working-class (youth) culture. Both approaches stress that much of the boys' activity is aimed at 'problem-solving' within limited constraints, and this should be kept in mind when interpreting *Figure 2*:

The major difference between Merton and the Marxists is that the former sees society as a system of conformity/non-conformity, whereas the latter see it as a system of dominance/subordination/resistance. The conformity/nonconformity (or deviance) framework persists in the work of all the American scholars with the exception of Miller, and even he has recently moved away from class analysis and emphasized the role of a variety of other factors, such as local urban environment, in explaining particular subcultural activity. Miller aside, the tendency of American writers to see youth subcultures in terms of deviance is radically different from the class perspective employed by the British Marxists. It is tempting to conclude that American sociologists have typically underestimated the role of class, and British Marxists have typically overestimated it. If so, there is a lot of theoretical reworking and reconciliation to do.

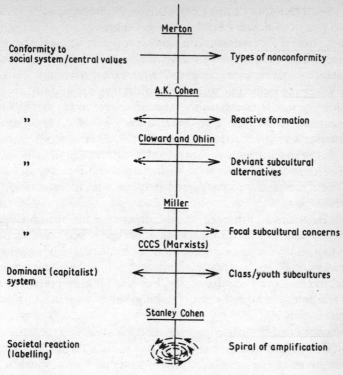

	Merton	
Conformity to social system/central values		Types of nonconformity
	A.K. Cohen	
"		Reactive formation
	Cloward and Ohlin	
"		Deviant subcultural alternatives
	Miller	
"		Focal subcultural concerns
	CCCS (Marxists)	
Dominant (capitalist) system		Class/youth subcultures
	Stanley Cohen	
Societal reaction (labelling)		Spiral of amplification

Note: The broken arrow head indicates a weaker flow of influence.

While fully acknowledging the role of social structural factors in forming youth subcultures, Stanley Cohen's (1972) particular concern is with societal reaction to them and how, by a complex process of social/subcultural interaction, the subcultures become 'created' and 'amplified' into more than they would otherwise have been. We can refer to this as the interactionist (or 'labelling') theory of deviance. Cohen traces the history of the mods and rockers of the 1960s from the initial identification of the issue, through the height of the 'moral panic', to the eventual decline of public concern. He emphasizes especially the role of the media in amplifying

71

deviant behaviour, and this point has also been taken up by Hebdige in *Subculture* (1979) and Stuart Hall *et al.* in *Policing the Crisis* (1978). In both cases, however, they stress that the selection of panics is related to the needs of the capitalist system at a given time (see Hebdige on 'incorporation'). Thus Hall sees the panic in the 1970s about mugging, and the race 'issue' generally, as symptomatic of a profound 'crisis' in capitalism. Panics serve to divert attention and energy from criticism and change of the system itself. Cohen also relates panics to social structure, but more broadly. For him, panics – whether in capitalist society or otherwise –indicate a sense of threat ('a boundary crisis') and play the role of reinforcing consensus.

Stanley Cohen has been mainly responsible for introducing the labelling theory of deviance (and deviant subcultures) into Britain. The following quotation from Jack Douglas and Frances Waksler locates this approach within the American theories we have been discussing, but it can play a similar role in relation to linking the structural and subcultural in Marxist theory too:

'Perhaps the major insight of subcultural theory is that different and at times conflicting values may exist within a society when one part of society (generally the one that embodies the defining values of that society) is able to establish rules that apply to everyone, other parts (including subcultures) come to be labelled deviant. Subcultural theory did not explore this process in any great detail; it remained for the labelling theorists ... to explain how this process "creates" deviance and deviants. Subcultural theory, however, did set the stage for undermining the *assumptions* of societal homogeneity and moral absolution.'

(Douglas and Waksler 1982: 90)

Activities

1 Select one area of social life (e.g. education, leisure). Show the extent to which the values and actions of 'the lads' reflect those of the traditional working class.

2 Discuss to what extent Marxist youth subcultural theory and 'American' subcultural theory are complementary.

Further reading

There is no shortage of good material in this area. The introductory essay in Hall and Jefferson (1976) is probably still the best overview of the subject, despite the reservations I make above. Hebdige (1979) blends Marxism and semiology and remains highly readable, if occasionally demanding for younger students.

The topic of youth culture/subcultures is one which rewards acquaintance with original materials. O'Donnell (1983), section 6, 'Youth (and Class)' contains extracts from functionalist and Marxist-subcultural perspectives. Readings 15 (Paul Willis), 51 (Albert Cohen), and 53 (Stanley Cohen) are also directly relevant. I recommend two articles on girls and subcultures: McRobbie and Garber (1976), and McRobbie (1978a).

4

Black youth

Blacks and British society

The experience of black youth in Britain needs to be understood in the context of a number of factors. First, the nature of British society and particularly the attitudes of the indigenous inhabitants to black immigrants and their offspring. Second, the cultures of the immigrants themselves, who are predominantly Afro-Caribbean or Asian. Third, the interaction of the first two factors in the form of the various responses of immigrant ethnic groups, especially their younger members, to their experience in Britain.

In the 1950s there was widespread support within Britain, as well as the black Commonwealth, for a multiracial Commonwealth of equal citizens. This sentiment was based on practical economic as well as idealistic motives. In the postwar period of economic expansion, Britain needed to increase its labour force and both public and private sectors actively recruited workers in the black Commonwealth. Blacks often took low-paid, monotonous jobs in heavy industry or transport, which indigenous workers preferred not to do. This enabled many of the latter to move up into white-collar employment. However, racial tension was not long in appearing. The most serious early examples were the race riots of 1958 in Notting Hill, London, and several other cities. A substantial body of opinion began to be heard in favour of reducing black immigration. Britain's still buoyant demand for labour could be met by European migrant workers, and the 1960s saw the gradual stripping away of the rights of immigration of Commonwealth citizens. The 1971 Immigration Act replaced the status of immigrant worker with that of temporary (but possibly renewable) migrant worker. Since then, legislation has been passed to reduce the rate of immigration of the kith and kin of established immigrants. The zeal with which immigration officials and the police have tended to enforce Britain's now strict immigration laws has caused friction with the black community.

Over roughly the same period that immigration was made more difficult, a series of Race Relations Acts was passed, making discrimination unlawful in public places, and including employment, housing, accommodation, and the provision of goods, facilities, and services in general. To promote racial harmony further, the Commission for Racial Equality was set up in 1976 and local Community Relations Councils were established.

However, it is much easier to state the legal principle of racial equality than it is to enforce it. Despite the above legislation, there is ample evidence to show that discrimination against blacks continues on a wide scale. Discrimination is probably most damaging in the employment market. In a survey published in 1977 (Smith 1977), the Political and Economic Planning group reported substantial discrimination occurring in the market for manual jobs: West Indians (27 per cent of cases); Indians (28 per cent); and Pakistanis (23 per cent). Other research suggests that, in the case of applications for white-collar jobs, discrimination against West Indian and Asian applicants occurred in about 30 per cent of cases. In this crucial area for advancement, then, substantial discrimination exists.

Discrimination aside, immigrant groups invariably face problems of adjustment to a new society of both a material and a cultural nature. These vary in kind and degree between ethnic groups. The West Indian immigrants of the 1950s and 1960s were predominantly lower class, and they often found it difficult to give their children effective support in education and the pursuit of a career in an alien society. Arguably, too, many first- and second-generation West Indian children have been disadvantaged by the one-parent family system common in the black communities of the West Indies and Britain. Asian immigrants came from a variety of socio-economic backgrounds but the majority took low-paying jobs when they came to Britain. A substantial minority was helped by the strong tradition of small business within the Asian community. Asian culture generally, and the typically close-knit Asian family, have tended to be strongly supportive of educational and, for boys, career aspirations.

The majority of blacks, then, have suffered a convergence of racial and class disadvantage in Britain. Despite this, most black immigrants have got on with what they came to Britain to do – find jobs and build a satisfying life. Race relations have been aggravated by high rates of unemployment, however, and the recession has affected black employment particularly badly and black youth employment worst of all. This undoubtedly contributed to the deterioration in race relations in the late 1970s and early 1980s.

The 'objective reality' of racial disadvantage in the various spheres of British life is difficult to measure. Just as important in analysing race in Britain, however, is understanding what people *think* about the extent of racism. *Table 5* provides comparative data, not on racial disadvantage, but on changing attitudes to race relations. The two samples were taken in 1981

Table 5   *Race relations in the country as a whole*

| | ethnic minorities | | | | | | whites | |
| | all | | W. Indians | | Asians | | all | |
	1981 %	1975 %	1981 %	1975 %	1981 %	1975 %	1981 %	1975 %
better	18	44	17	46	16	43	25	32
same	28	31	25	26	33	33	35	37
worse	47	13	52	16	43	11	33	20
don't know	7	12	6	12	8	12	7	10
no. of respondents	1,057	966	370	324	330	584	1,073	1,050

Note: Because of rounding, not all total percentages add up to 100.
Source: Adapted from Commission for Racial Equality (1981: 14, Table 16).

and 1975 by a research team under the auspices of the Commission for Racial Equality (previously the Community Relations Commission). The title of the report was *Race Relations in 1981: An Attitude Survey*, and it compared the attitudes of ethnic minorities to those of whites. The total ethnic minority sample in both years contained responses from Chinese, Africans, Cypriots, and 'others', as well as from West Indians and Asians (whose responses are presented separately as well as included in the main ethnic group sample).

The survey shows that in 1981 nearly half of the ethnic minority respondents and almost a third of the whites thought race relations were worsening in Britain. As the report puts it, this 'situation is dramatically different from that revealed in the 1975 survey', especially in the case of the ethnic minorities. The survey was taken before the summer disturbances of 1981 but it foreshadows what was to come.

West Indian immigrants: class and cultural formations

Before considering black youth in detail, it will help to sketch out the position of West Indian immigrants in British society with reference to both class and cultural factors. We can then locate black youth more precisely within the wider ethnic framework. *Figure 3* should be regarded as no more than an ideal-type guide to a much more complex reality. It is derived from Ken Pryce's presentation of black life styles in Bristol in *Endless Pressure* (1979: 271). Pryce's categorization has caused some debate and I simply use it as a useful descriptive starting-point, without making any theoretical assumptions (theoretical issues will be raised later). I have also departed from Pryce's terminology in three minor respects. First, whereas he refers to 'those who work' and 'those who don't work', I use the terms 'black employed' and 'black unemployed'. In some respects the term 'black non-employed' is better than 'black unemployed', because it indicates more clearly that some members of this group do not seek employment in the formal economy. However I have used the term 'unemployed' because it is more familiar. Second, instead of the term 'young unemployed', Pryce uses 'teenyboppers'. I find this term rather dated. Third, I prefer the description 'black white-collar employees' to his 'mainliners'.

The above scheme embodies both class and ethnic cultural factors. As Pryce says, the majority of blacks fall into two major groups: the employed black working class and the unemployed, some of whom are hustlers. There is a large proportion of hustlers among the young unemployed, and even

Figure 3 West Indian immigrants in British society: class and cultural factors

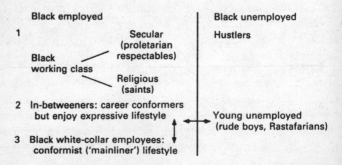

older school-children. Pryce divides the black working class into the proletarian respectables, who are generally conformist and ambitious, especially for their children, and the 'saints' who spend a considerable part of their leisure time involved in fundamentalist religion. In this respect they are like their relatives in Jamaica, a basically Protestant country in which a variety of cults proliferate among the lower class. The saints find expression through religion – especially in gospel music and the sermon – and a focus for social life in the local church. The other two employed groups, the in-betweeners and white-collar employees, account for a relatively small minority of the West Indian ethnic community. Astonishingly, Pryce was unable to find a single case of a higher professional West Indian in Bristol in the early 1970s, although routine white-collar employees were not uncommon.

West Indian youth: education, employment/unemployment, and size of generational cohort

Most young blacks conform both in the sense that they observe the law and share (with their white peers) a desire for 'a good life'. Their major problem is that they experience more obstacles to achieving it. Or, in the more formal language of American subcultural theory, the legitimate opportunity structure is, if not quite closed, nearly so. Nevertheless, even in the recession-hit Britain of the mid-1980s, most young people of West Indian extraction either have jobs or are seriously looking for one. It is easy to forget this in the face of common stereotypes of black youth as workshy and delinquent. Nevertheless, as we shall shortly see, unemployment is a bigger problem for black youth than almost any other section of the population.

Educational success is one means to social advancement, although not a guarantee in times of recession. *Table 6* shows that, compared to young Asians and others, young blacks have been obtaining much poorer qualifications.

These general statistics hide two important factors. First, there is an increasing body of research which suggests that it is the low socio-economic status of the parents of most black pupils that explains their educational performance rather than ethnic cultural or racial reasons. In 1971, Bagley matched fifty West Indian primary school-children who had been fully educated in Britain with fifty English children. He was testing the hypothesis that black children from stable working-class or lower middle-class homes would not be intellectually disadvantaged. The West Indian children averaged slightly higher

Table 6 *School leavers: achievements, destinations, and further education*

	Asians	West Indians	all other leavers	all maintained school leavers in England
CSE and O level achievements	%	%	%	%
no graded results (includes those attempting)	19	17	22	14
at least 1 graded result but less than 5 higher grades	63	81	62	66
5 or more higher grades	18	3	16	21
Destination of school leavers				
university	3	1	3	5
other further education	18	16	9	14
employment	54	65	77	74
unknown	25	18	11	8
Full-time further education courses				
degree	5	1	4	6
A level	6	2	1	2
any other course	11	15	7	11
no course (including unknown destination)	78	83	88	81
total (number)	527	799	4,852	693,840

Note: All figures refer to leavers in six local education authorities.
Source: Rampton Report (1981).

scores than the English, 105 to 103. These results supported the view that social class factors are paramount in explaining the underachievement of black pupils.

Current research is also producing interesting data on the educational performance of West Indian girls relative to West Indian boys. As many as a dozen studies now indicate that the girls do rather better than the boys. For instance, Mary Fuller (1982) found that in the 'academic' band of the fifth form of a mixed comprehensive school, black girls averaged 7.6 'O' level and CSE exam passes as against 5.6 for the black boys. Fuller's study is full of illuminating detail. She says of the girls that they 'formed a discernible subculture within the school'. This emerged 'from the girls' positive acceptance of the fact of being black and female'. They were committed to achieving academic success but were not pro-school. Academic and ultimately career success were necessary both materially and psychologically: the first because many black women have to be major breadwinners, the second to give them a sense of self-worth. However, they had no normative commitment to general conformity at school. There are three aspects to this attitude. First, to appear too keen might attract the ridicule of black boys with whom they saw themselves as partly in competition. Second, their self-image tended to be that of fun-lovers not 'goody-goodies'. Third, they realized that public examinations were not assessed by their teachers.

The independence and resourcefulness of the girls reflects the role of women in West Indian culture, both in the Caribbean and in Britain. As Fuller says, this culture is not matriarchal, in the sense of female dominated, but it is largely matrifocal in that the women's domestic labour, often combined with employment in the job market, is the major basis of family life and stability. The number of one-parent families and the high rate of male unemployment contribute to this. West Indian girls, it seems, are used to coping.

All young blacks, whatever their qualifications, run the risk of discrimination in the job market. As we saw, the risk is quite high on a percentage basis. The low qualifications of most young blacks make matters worse. The CRE survey (1981) referred to above found that 58 per cent of young West Indians, aged 18–24, had been unemployed at some point and looking for work for a month or more. This compared to 42 per cent of young ethnic minorities in general and 36 per cent for all young people. Estimates of black youth unemployment during the recession range between about 20 and 30 per cent, and even higher in deindustrialized, inner-urban areas. In the area covered by the Brixton Employment Office the rate of young blacks registered as unemployed in 1981 was 55 per cent. This still leaves uncounted the unregistered unemployed! Of course, these global figures are made up partly of different young blacks moving in and out of employment, although from 1971 long-term unemployment of six months, a year, or longer has become increasingly common, especially among blacks (Scarman 1982: 27). A majority of young blacks, then, have experienced unemployment and many frequently or for lengthy periods of time. Some young blacks virtually stop looking for a job after repeated disappointments, but many more continue to use Job Centres or careers offices. Either way, they still have to occupy their time. We shall return to how they do so shortly.

It is worth noting that, because of the age structure of the black population in Britain, there are large numbers of young people relative to the rest of the black population. This is because the black immigrants of the 1950s and 1960s tended to be young adults who, in due course, produced children. As teenagers in the 1970s and 1980s, these offspring achieved a high visibility in British life, not least because of their liking for street culture. By contrast, there were relatively many fewer blacks of over fifty-five. This untypical population structure will work itself out by the year 2000, when the total black population in Britain (all of New Commonwealth and Pakistan ethnic origin) is estimated to stabilize at around 6 per cent of the total population. However, the point to note here is the relatively large and prominent presence of young blacks in the 1970s and 1980s.

Activities

1 What differences are there in the experiences and attitudes of the first postwar generation of West Indian immigrants, and their children and grandchildren?

2 Why do you think some West Indian girls have a particular commitment to educational and employment success, and a general capacity to 'cope with life'?

Black (West Indian) youth subcultures

The difficulties that many young blacks face at school and in getting work mean that large numbers of them drift into ethnic youth subcultures. The life style of these subcultures involves at least as much 'resistance' to the dominant system as do working-class youth subcultures. The following extract from the *Scarman Report* refers specifically to the young blacks of Brixton, but it is applicable to similar inner-urban areas such as Toxteth, Liverpool, and Moss Side, Manchester:

'*The young people of Brixton: a people of the street*

Many of the young people of Brixton are therefore born and raised in insecure social and economic conditions, and in an impoverished physical environment. They share the desires and expectations which our materialist society encourages. At the same time, many of them fail to achieve educational success and on leaving school face the stark prospect of unemployment. Many of these difficulties face white as well as black youngsters, but it is clear that they bear particularly heavily on young blacks. In addition, young black people face the burden of discrimination, much of it hidden and some of it unconscious and unintended. Without close parental support, with no job to go to, and with few recreational facilities available, the young black person makes his life on the streets and in the seedy, commercially run clubs of Brixton. There he meets criminals, who appear to have no difficulty in obtaining the benefits of a materialist society. The process was described to me in evidence by the Railton Road Youth and Community Centre as follows:

"Young people around in the streets all day, with nothing to do and nowhere to go, get together in groups and the 'successful' criminal has a story to tell. So one evil has bred another, and as unemployment has grown in both older and younger generations crime has become more commonplace and more acceptable. This is a vicious circle to which there is no present end in sight.'"

(Scarman 1982: 28–9)

The extract gives a good thumb-nail sketch of the social conditions in which many young blacks make their lives. However, we should not let Lord Scarman's concern with law and order lead to a misunderstanding about the place of criminality in black youth subculture. Music, 'blues' (dances), Rastafarian religion and dress, are all part of their life style. For some, theft and petty crime are one way of sustaining it – and so they become a part of the life style itself. To label their subcultural activity deviant, as American subcultural theorists might, is to miss the wider point.

The major subcultural life styles open to young black males are those of hustler or Rastafarian, although in practice overlap occurs frequently. It helps to regard the two life styles as patterns of behaviour available for imitation and, of course, further development.

The hustler lives off his wits. Unable to get a job or rejecting 'slave labour' as humiliating, boring, and badly paid, he sees little option but to break the law to make money. From the mid-1960s one popular model for the young hustler was the Jamaican 'rude boy'. Originally, the rudies resembled white skinheads in both attitudes and dress. Indeed, the two groups sometimes acted together in the 1960s to terrorize young Asians. Knowledge of and, ideally, prowess in music – 'ska', then 'steady rock' – were important in the rudies' style and image. 'Sharper', slicker varieties of rude boys developed, whose status depended on money, appearance, and conspicuous consumption. Pushing 'dope', dealing in stolen goods, cheque frauds, gambling, stealing, and pimping are possible ways of hustling. The high-status rude boy must be willing occasionally to be tough, as well as smooth – for instance, over disputes about 'dealing rights' in a given territory. Inevitably, many rude boys fall short of their own standards. Social security, which some despise, nevertheless remains an option for 'hard times'.

Ernest Cashmore suggests that the small gang structure of eight to twelve members, laid down by the rudies, provided a basis for later Rastafarian organization. The Rastafarian life style also first flourished in the West Indies. It was originally gentler and more 'laid back' than that of the rudies. Rastafarianism is a religious cult movement whose members adopt a system of beliefs which stresses the virtue and potential for salvation of the black race. The original inspiration behind the movement was Marcus Garvey, who was a prominent campaigner for black rights in the United States and the West Indies in the 1920s. Disillusioned with racism in America, he began to preach for a return to Africa. He is supposed to have uttered the prophetic words: 'Look to Africa when a black king shall be crowned, for the day of deliverance is near.' Although Garvey believed 'God has no colour', he urged blacks to 'believe in the God of Ethiopia' and to see the world through 'black spectacles'.

The crowning of the Prince Regent, Ras Tafari, as Emperor of Ethiopia in November 1930 was widely taken in Jamaica to vindicate Garvey. The Emperor was officially titled Haile Selassie I, King of Kings, Lord of Lords, the all-conquering Lion of the Tribe of Judah, and known internationally as Emperor Haile Selassie. Apart from extolling the virtues of blacks and the evil of whites, the Rastafarians followed Garvey in advocating a return to the Ethiopian fatherland. They awaited only the word of their redeemer, the divine Haile Selassie.

It is easy to see why such a philosophy of hope should appeal to lower-class Jamaicans, victimized as they were by racism and poverty. Ernest Cashmore, who has made a detailed study of the Rastafarian movement (1979), suggests three main reasons or 'principal motivational routes' which lead mainly lower-class blacks to Rastafarianism: 'the need for identity, the need for explanation, and the need for mobilization' (getting organized).

These motivations apply, particularly to younger blacks, in contemporary Jamaica and Britain as much as they did in the 1930s. The 'Rasta' identity lies in exalting and rejoicing in being black. The 'Rasta' explanation is that blacks are the 'lost tribe', held in captivity in 'Babylon' (the white-dominated west), who will one day return to the promised land (Ethiopia). Something of the flavour of Rastafarian beliefs can be gleaned in the following extract from the song, 'Rivers of Babylon' (note: 'King Alfa' is presumably Emperor Haile Selassie):

'By the rivers of Babylon
Where he sat down,
And there he went
When he remembered Zion.
But the wicked carried us away captivity,
Require from us a song,
How can we sing King Alfa song
In a strange land.'

It conveys the misery of downtrodden exile, but Rastafarianism gives hope for the future as well as help to bear present suffering. The hope is the restoration of the blacks to their rightful position, the return to the promised land. This provides a motive for action or 'mobilization' – albeit a remote one.

The above, largely descriptive, material partly explains the Rastafarian movement in Britain, but more specific sociological comment is also needed. First, John Rex (1982) is right when he says: 'Young men (and women) do not normally turn to religious movements for explanation of their rejection and their deviance.' In other words, things have to be bad before young people will turn away from society (Babylon), and seek their meaning and life style in a radical religion.

Second, whereas Rex indicates what young black Rastafarians are reacting against, Ernest Cashmore emphasizes the positive nature of their response and its links with West Indian traditions:

'Ras Tafari was a creative response to confusion within the second-generation West Indian community. After experiencing difficulty and anxiety in trying to make satisfactory sense of what were considered to be important matters of existence, they turned to the comprehensive world view of Rasta where they found fulfilments of their need for an understanding of the world and their place in that world, as well as a vehicle for mobilizing sentiments and reinforcing black solidarity'.   (Cashmore 1979: 69)

Third, the significance of the fact that young blacks have so far found their major collective expression in an alternative cultural/religious movement rather than in a political one is worth exploring in detail. Cultural movements are expressed primarily through life style, whereas political movements aim at acquiring power and affecting policies. The advantage for members of cultural movements is that they can avoid directly confronting what they oppose in society. They are able simultaneously to retreat from the dominant society and yet show and even celebrate their difference from it through style and ritual. Adopting dreadlocks and Ethiopian-coloured garments is joyful protest, at once safe but conspicuous. Language is the core of culture and sometimes young blacks use Creole (a West Indian dialect of English) to distance themselves from the dominant system, for instance, at school or in dealings with the police. The disadvantage of cultural protest is that it is likely to leave intact the power structure and social system that produce marginality. By contrast, political action confronts the issues of power and policy directly. This directness may result in the political movement being more effective, or it may be defeated by opinion or suppressed by force.

Cultural movements tend to be fluid and ill defined, so they can sustain a great variety of behaviour and opinions. So we find Rastas who combine their religion with socialist beliefs, and others who adopt Rastafarianism in no more than appearance – so-called 'pseud-Rastas'. Shiva Naipaul describes this diversity well, if unsympathetically:

'No theology is more fluid, more elusive. There is no church; there are no scriptures; there is no ordained leadership. Each Rastafarian has his own version of the thing. You become a Rastafarian by declaring yourself to be such – or simply, by beginning to look like one. There are those who call themselves Rastafarian and who abhor ganja. Ganja is derived from marijuana, and is a sacred substance to many Rastafarians. Some reject the divinity of Selassie. The brethren can be "clean-faced" or dreadlocked. Many are socialist and many are not. Some are primitivist in outlook, some drive around in sports cars and travel between continents by jet plane.'   (Naipaul 1982)

Naipaul makes no secret of the fact that he finds contemporary Rastafarianism formless and often superficial. Certainly, there are those who merely flirt with the movement. But, as Cashmore says, for others it has provided and still provides a flexible point of reference and identity. Given the weakness of black politics in Britain, it is difficult to see from where else this might have come. The 'host nation' itself did not provide an adequate alternative.

Young West Indians have adjusted to (or negotiated with) the system of life in Britain mainly through culture rather than politics. Sometimes 'adjustment' has collapsed into escapism or sparked into spontaneous resistance (see p. 91). Nevertheless, organized black political or trade union activity has occurred. I shall deal with both West Indian and Asian youth politics below. Here it will be useful to examine a particular example of a primarily political rather than cultural response to racial oppression, involving mainly young people of West Indian origin. The Californian-based Black Panther Party, founded in the mid-1960s, provides an excellent case for comparison with the Rastafarian movement. (A directly political manifestation of the black power movement did occur in Britain, in which Michael X was a prominent figure, but this was not on a comparable scale to the Panthers.)

The Black Panther Party of the United States ran community programmes, published a newspaper, and armed themselves for 'community self-defence against the police'. Their ideology contained elements of black 'nationalism' and Marxism. To focus the comparison with the Rastafarians, we will analyse the Panthers in terms of the three motives Cashmore indicates for the former movement: the needs for identity, explanation, and mobilization. These needs were felt as acutely by young, urban blacks in America in the 1960s as by their counterparts in contemporary Britain.

The Panthers used powerful symbols to assert their black identity. For instance, they wore a paramilitary uniform. The term 'black power' is itself a statement of identity. Chanted as a slogan, to the accompaniment of a raised, clenched fist, it conveyed a message of black strength and solidarity through the world media. As well as being rendered powerless, blacks in the United States had often been made to feel dirty and ugly. The slogan 'black is beautiful', used by the Panthers, denied the insult and re-established a positive self-image.

Like Rastafarianism, the Black Panthers offered an explanation for the exploitation of blacks. Their ideological analysis was that the majority of blacks suffered a dual subordination, class and racial, which reflected the capitalist and racist nature of American society. They never fully reconciled their uneasy blend of Marxism and black nationalism, and this ideological tension contributed to a split in the party. On the one hand, Stokely Carmichael opted for an extreme 'return to Africa', nationalist solution, whereas Eldridge Cleaver began to talk seriously of violent, socialist revolution in the United States.

We now come to Cashmore's third motivational need – mobilization. In this respect, there is a crucial difference between political and religious movements: the former requires practical action in the here and now, whereas the latter can defer solutions to the hereafter. The Black Panthers sought black mobilization to achieve a political and social revolution. Their statements on the role of violence in bringing about revolution are not always consistent or clear, but they certainly used the rhetoric of violence to an extreme degree. Whether or not David Hilliard, a West Coast Panther, expected his threat in 1969 that 'the Panthers ... will kill Nixon, or anyone who stands in the way of black people's freedom' to be taken seriously, such statements put the Panthers in direct conflict with the police and the Federal Bureau of Investigation. It was a confrontation they were bound to lose. At the turn of the decade several Panthers were killed or severely injured in a series of shoot-outs with the police. A number received lengthy prison sentences. The Panthers were finished as an effective force, though the black power movement has achieved a broad and continuing influence.

The key difference between the Black Panther Party and the Rastafarian movement is that the former attempted to bring about change by direct and potentially violent political action, whereas the latter provides an alternative way of being for blacks without bringing them into immediate confrontation with the forces of law and order. In this case the Rastafarian approach has proved the safer – because it need never really be tested. There is a comparison here between Rastafarianism and apocalyptical religious groups. When the latter fail to prophesy the end of the world correctly, they can merely recalculate the date. Similarly, the Rastas can defer indefinitely the 'real solution' – return to Africa. Indeed, the Jamaican wing of the movement has survived the fiasco of at least one mass repatriation which failed to materialize on the appointed day.

The advantage, admittedly unintended, of Rastafarianism is that it avoids confrontation with the overwhelming resources of the power structure; the disadvantage is that it does little to change it. It is, of course, the necessary role of political action to achieve such change. The comparison with the Panthers is not intended, therefore, as an argument against political action. It simply points out the dangers of revolutionary politics in an unrevolutionary situation. We return to the important issue of political action later.

The urban disorders of 1981

'1.2 During the weekend of 10–12 April (Friday, Saturday, and Sunday) the British people watched with horror and incredulity an instant audio-visual presentation on their television sets of scenes of violence and disorder in their capital city, the like of which had not previously been seen in this century in Britain. In the centre of Brixton, a few hundred young people – most, but not all of them, black – attacked the police on the streets with stones, bricks, iron bars, and petrol bombs, demonstrating to millions of their fellow citizens the fragile basis of the Queen's peace.'

(Scarman 1982: 13)

The opening sentences of the Scarman Report describe what was, indeed, an awesome experience for the British people. More disorders, of varying extent, were to follow in June and July of 1981. These occurred widely throughout England's urban centres, particularly those with large immigrant communities.

Why did the disturbances occur? In particular, why were young people the predominant participants in them? We must distinguish between the tinder and the spark or, more sociologically, the deep structural predispositions and the immediate causes. We can deal briefly with the former here, because we have already described them earlier in this chapter. The experiences of failure in education and the job market, relative poverty, and the pervasive possibility of racism combine to produce frustration among young blacks. The prospect of long-term unemployment in a society of conspicuous consumption no doubt contributed to the souring of those young whites who participated. In both cases, society had not delivered according to their best expectations and desires.

91

It is interesting to note that the attitude survey carried out by the Commission for Racial Equality in 1981 found that both whites and ethnic minorities tended to see unemployment as not only the most important problem, but as rapidly worsening. *Table 7* gives details. The massive loss of belief in the availability of work clearly reflected the recession of the early 1980s. That 67 per cent of ethnic minorities (80 per cent of West Indians) thought availability was 'bad or very bad' represents a crisis of confidence. There was no simple cause-effect relationship between unemployment and the urban disorders, but the logic of Lord Scarman's rueful reflections on the options open to young unemployed blacks quoted above is irrefutable. Scarman was wise after the event, but the following two middle-aged male respondents, a Cypriot and an Asian respectively, perhaps had premonitions:

'Unemployment – nowhere for the young unemployed to go, nothing for them to do except get into trouble.'   (Cypriot)
'Unemployment, youngsters are getting violent, and making trouble to keep their minds occupied.'   (Asian)

Table 7   *Ratings of facilities in the area – employment*

	ethnic minorities				whites	
	all	all	W. Indians	Asians	all	all
	1981 %	1975 %	1981 %	1981 %	1981 %	1975 %
availability of work						
good or very good	8	46	4	11	16	46
neither good nor bad	12	16	7	15	18	20
bad or very bad	67	25	80	61	58	22
don't know/no answer	13	13	8	13	9	12

Notes: Comparative data for 1975 for West Indians and Asians were not available.
Because of rounding, not all total percentages add up to 100.
Source: Commission for Racial Equality (1981: 7, Table 6).

It is important to interpret the attitudes of young West Indians precisely. George Gaskell and Patten Smith's (1981) article 'Are Young Blacks Really Alienated?' helps us to do so. In the winter of 1979–80, they interviewed 240 young men in London between the ages of 16 and 25, the majority of whom were West Indian. Some of the West Indians were employed, others not. They were able to provide substantial evidence to undermine two common stereotypes about the attitudes of young West Indians. First, they found little to support the hypothesis that young West Indian males are generally alienated from British society. Black and white, employed and unemployed alike, shared a desire for a good job, material possessions, marriage, and a family. A second hypothesis they found little support for was that young blacks are unrealistic in their job expectations. Most of the unemployed would have settled for the manual jobs that in better times they would probably have got.

What Gaskell and Smith did find were feelings of deprivation, hopelessness, and despair (experiences more akin to anomie than to conscious alienation). At a certain point of frustration or provocation such attitudes can lead to angry and hostile behaviour. In referring to the Brixton disorders, they write:

'Besides hostility towards the police, our research suggests that high levels of deprivation, both objective and subjective, combined with the degree of hopelessness and despair felt by the blacks of Brixton, were important contributory factors. Unless these social deprivations are lessened, and community policing organized which has the confidence of the ethnic minorities, further episodes like Brixton must be expected.'
(Gaskell and Smith 1984: 261)

The immediate cause of both the Brixton and several other major disturbances was the tense relations between the black community and the police. The *Scarman Report* gives several reasons for the hostility of young blacks towards the police, and the loss of confidence in them of significant sections of the

Lambeth public (Brixton is part of the London Borough of Lambeth): these included 'the collapse of the police liaison committee in 1979; "hard" policing methods which caused offence and apprehension to many; lack of consultation about police operations; distrust of the procedure for investigating complaints against the police; and unlawful and, in particular, racially prejudiced conduct by some police officers'. In fairness it must be said that the report is generally sympathetic to the police and condemns the illegal behaviour that occurred during the weekend.

Finally, at the level of immediate causation, a 'copy-cat' element in the spread of the disorders (other than Brixton) must be noted. The *Hytner Report* (Venner 1984) on the Moss Side disturbances in Manchester concludes that they occurred largely in imitation of the preceding outbreaks in Brixton, Southall, and Toxteth. Moss Side was no more deprived than some other areas of Manchester but it had a history and continuing reputation for being so. 'The myth of Moss Side' contributed to the build-up of expectations that violence would occur. When, on the morning of Wednesday 8 July, 1981, a group of white youths taunted some black youths that they were slow compared with their brethren in Brixton and Toxteth, violence duly broke out. This seems to be a good example of what Stanley Cohen calls the 'creation' of deviance, not only by the media but in this case by popular will and imagination.

It would be inappropriate to conclude this section on what is almost a comic note. Mary Venner (1984), who has commented on the Hytner Report, sets the matter straight: 'In uncovering the apparently trivial origins of the disturbances ... the report sheds light on pre-existing conditions which cannot with certainty be said to have caused the riots, but which have been revealed by them'.

After 'Brixton'

Writing just three years after the disorders of 1981, it is difficult to conclude that much has been done fundamentally to improve the conditions Venner refers to and which I described in relation to Brixton earlier in this chapter. A number of changes have been made in policing – some of them highly controversial – and a certain amount of 'extra' money has been directed towards inner-urban projects. However, the fundamental facts of high unemployment, especially among black youths, and inequality remain. Perhaps a government which believes that wealth is created in the private sector and distributed through the 'free market' is prevented by its own ideology from doing anything radical to change the conditions that underlay the disorders of 1981. John Rex and Sally Tomlinson (1979) write of continuing 'racial polarization' in Britain. They use the term 'black underclass' to describe the position of the majority of blacks. Marxists argue that this term distinguishes too sharply between the stratificational position of most blacks and lower working-class whites. Theoretical dispute aside, the facts of racism in Britain are obvious, destructive, and potentially disastrous.

Asian youth and racial victimization in Britain

In terms of educational (see *Table 6*) and occupational status, young Asians are generally in a better position than young West Indians. There are a number of reasons for this. One is the family stability and support provided in most Asian communities. Second is the quality of education and culture within such traditions as the Sikh, Hindu, and Islamic, which carries over into a keenness to make the most of British education. Third, a minority of Asians brought with them professional or business experience, and, in a few cases, some capital. These factors were an advantage to their children. Fourth, there is a tradition of hard work shared by many; it is said that Asians are responsible for reintroducing the sixteen-hour day into Britain! Nevertheless, Asians are generally poorer than whites, have lower-status occupations, and are liable to be the victims of racism.

Young Asians are in a different position from their parents. They do not expect to return to the 'homeland', unlike many of their parents, so the strength of their traditional cultures and the need to adjust successfully to British society require them 'to face in two directions'. This can cause acute and painful conflict. Perhaps the most tragic example of this is when daughter and parents cannot agree over an arranged marriage (a traditional practice of several Asian religions). On the other hand, those who do adjust successfully to the two cultures probably acquire useful social skills in doing so.

Were it not for white racism, it might be possible to be optimistic that most young Asians would successfully adjust and even prosper in Britain. It is therefore necessary briefly to consider the formidable obstacle that racism presents to many young Asians, as well as to West Indians. Racism against Asians, young and older, has had a peculiarly vicious aspect to it. *Blood on the Tracks*, published by the Bethnal Green and Stepney Trades Council, contains a grim list of scores of racial attacks, many against Asians, in the East End of London between early 1976 and mid-1978. Arguing that police protection was ineffectual, some Asian youths organized the defence of their own community.

Clearly, only a small minority of whites would support such brutal actions. But is such behaviour the tip of the iceberg of racial prejudice in Britain, or wholly untypical? The evidence is contradictory. Only one National Front supporter has saved his deposit in a general election in Britain since the war. Attitude surveys consistently show 'only' around 10 per cent of the population as genuinely prejudiced. This was the figure produced by the Abrams Survey (1966; see Pilkington 1984), but it also found another 17 per cent were 'prejudice inclined'. Twenty-seven per cent of the population is large enough to make matters thoroughly difficult for blacks in major areas of public life. Commenting on racial attitudes in the 1980s, Rex and Tomlinson (1979) argue that Thatcherism has pre-empted the significant fascist resurgence of the late 1970s by adopting tough, right-wing policies on immigration and inner-urban law and order, and by ignoring racial inequality. It is uncomfortably difficult to be sure what degree of prejudice and oppression against blacks British public opinion might now tolerate.

This is not the place to suggest strategies for improving the conditions of blacks and the prospects for black youth in this country. The answer must involve political action by blacks at the ethnic community level and across class lines. Above all, the employment situation of most young blacks requires radical action. For all its wonderful creativity, the subcultural 'solution' alone is not solution enough.

Activities

1 Make a semiological analysis of black youth culture.
2 Discuss what or who you think caused the Brixton disorders of 10–12 April, 1981.

Further reading

There is a growing body of material on race suitable for the student reader. Pilkington (1984) is a good introduction. Cashmore and Troyna (1982) contains several useful contributions; particularly recommended is Mary Fuller's 'Young, Female, and Black'. Cashmore's own Rastaman *(1979) makes fascinating reading. There is a lot of interesting coverage of black youth in Pryce (1979), while the* Scarman Report *(1982) is highly affordable.*

5

Middle-class youth subcultures: the 1960s

The political and cultural youth movements of the 1960s are the subject of this chapter. I shall begin by giving a brief historical account of the main events and developments. Second, using historical and sociological perspectives, I shall attempt to explain why the movements occurred. Third, I shall try to establish what type or kind of movement, taken as a whole, it was. The term 'movement' will be used to refer to various radical political and cultural groups active in the 1960s. Most of the activists were middle class and young, but many were not.

Historical outline

We will examine the movement in the United States and then in Britain, in each case dealing first with the political and then the cultural wing.

The initial stirrings of youthful protest occurred in the United States in 1960–61. Two issues focused the attention of young people, especially students: the black civil rights movement for racial equality in the southern States, and the threat of nuclear war. In the south, the immediate aim was to desegregate public facilities, i.e. to achieve equality of access for blacks to such places as coffee bars, libraries, and toilets. The tactic they used was for groups, usually of both blacks and whites, to breach the practice of desegregation. The philosophy they adopted was that of non-violent protest extending, in some cases, to civil disobedience. Students from all over the United States took part in the civil rights movement – first in tens, then in hundreds. There were some demonstrations about the nuclear threat in the early 1960s, but these were superseded in the mid-1960s by growing mass concern about the Vietnam War. Anti-Vietnam War protest was only partly generationally based but young people had to fight the war (over 50,000 young American males died in it), and this sharpened their involvement.

A third issue in the early 1960s was of specific interest to students but had wider implications. Students increasingly questioned the paternalistic authority structure of the universities and, as they saw it, the impersonal and bureaucratic way in which they were run. The paternalism was fairly easily swept aside in the new, permissive climate and university rules were widely liberalized. However, the large-scale, alienating nature of the administration (and even the teaching) of some of the larger universities was a less tractable problem. It reflected the issue of the 'little' individual against the 'big' organization, general in advanced industrial society. What the activists sought was a sense of community, but they felt as though they were being educationally 'processed'.

By 1966 the movement had clearly begun to change. Black power challenged the non-violent philosophy of civil rights. The paramilitary Black Panther Party adopted a revolutionary and quasi-Marxist ideology. In the late 1960s, a group of white activists established a revolutionary organization they called

'The Weathermen', which argued for the overthrow of United States capitalism and imperialism, blew up selected targets (buildings but not people), and robbed a number of banks to acquire funds. The more pacific ideas of the movement found expression primarily within its cultural wing, which we now examine.

In the early 1960s there was no conscious split between political and cultural radicalism. For instance, Bob Dylan's civil rights protest song, 'Blowing in the Wind', seemed to voice a widespread mood. As the decade progressed, however, a body of opinion developed which argued that social change could best be achieved not through the exercise of political power but by adopting 'alternative' personal and group life styles. To 'do it', as activist Jerry Rubin's slogan had it, was the best way to show it *could* be done. This sentiment partly inspired the commune movement and the nationwide flowering of an underground press. The idea also emerged that changing 'consciousness' was more important than changing 'structures'. Again, this meant a revolution of thought and life style which, it was believed, would lead to social and political (structural) change. Some thought that the quickest if not necessarily the most effective way to change consciousness was by using psychedelic drugs; others adopted philosophies such as Zen, either in whole or in part. The term counterculture refers to the above tendencies. At their most optimistic, members of the counterculture believed they could oppose (counter) dominant values and life styles, and gradually change them by example.

I will deal more sketchily with the political and cultural movements in Britain. This is because both the issues and the historical phases were similar to those in the United States, though the scale of involvement was less. Perhaps the major difference between the radical movements in the two countries was the race issue's lack of impact in Britain. In the early 1960s the nuclear issue was more prominent in Britain than the United States, largely because of the efforts of the Campaign for Nuclear Disarmament which had considerable youthful

100

support. From 1965 onwards support for the anti-Vietnam War movement built up in Britain, and between 1967 and 1968 there were three marches which ended with mass protests outside the United States embassy in London's Grosvenor Square.

1968 was the year the movement reached its height in the United States and Europe. In the parks of Chicago, radicals 'acted out' an alternative convention to that of the Democratic Party, which was meeting in the city to elect its presidential candidate. In France an uneasy alliance of students and workers briefly posed a very real threat to the government of General de Gaulle. The Angry Brigade was the British parallel to the Weathermen. It never reformed after the trial of some of its members in 1972. In West Germany, the Baader-Meinhof group mounted a better organized and more sustained policy of revolutionary terrorism against 'the capitalist state'. Only a small minority of activists in Europe and the United States opted for the politics of violent revolution. In general the movement began to fragment in the early 1970s, following the withdrawal of United States troops from Vietnam, and as the activists of the 1960s began to move into careers and adult commitments.

The scale of the counterculture in Britain was never comparable to that of the United States. This is partly because the higher education student population in the United States is at least ten times larger than Britain's — they are a larger proportion of a larger population. A student movement in the United States, therefore, has the potential to be both effective and dramatically visible. Nevertheless, there was certainly a 'hippie-type' element on and even beyond the British university campuses in the late 1960s, and the influence of British 'pop culture' was international. The Beatles were not taken with quite such philosophical seriousness as Bob Dylan, but they, the Rolling Stones, and other British groups were seen as symbols of a new, permissive, and adventurous life style. They contributed to the widely shared sense that 'something different' was happening.

Why did the movement 'happen'?

To understand why the movement occurred we need to examine the postwar political and cultural context, especially in the United States. The political climate was dominated by the Cold War. In the United States and western Europe it was widely accepted that Russian communism presented a threat to the west against which the possession of nuclear arms was a necessary protection. The student movement helped to raise questions on the possible contributions of the west to the Cold War and about the nuclear issue. Culturally, the mood of the first ten postwar years was conformist and businesslike. One commentator referred to students in the United States in this period as 'the silent generation'. Renata Adler (1970) observed of her student contemporaries: 'Everyone looked alike or tried to, every sort of maverick was cut off and lost.' Both the political and the cultural climates of the early and middle 1950s were so cautious and careful that a radical reaction, however modest, could almost have been predicted. Karl Mannheim suggests that such swings of opinion are normal from generation to generation. In fact, there were in any case developments occurring likely to facilitate such a swing of the political-cultural barometer.

Before dealing with the factors which specifically contributed to the student movement, it is worth recalling that relative affluence and the development of a mass market made a life style of reasonably colourful and comfortable consumption widely available. Postwar austerity was short-lived. Politically, there was a swing to more liberal options. In the United States, John Kennedy seemed to many to represent a new, progressive era and rather later, in Britain, Harold Wilson attempted to present himself somewhat similarly.

Several factors served to put students at the centre of this emerging situation of high confidence and expectation. First, in both Britain and the United States there was a huge expansion of higher education. New universities were founded, including Kent, Sussex, and Essex, and the older ones

102

increased their intake. In the United States, the number of students in higher education increased from about two million in 1950 to five million in 1960, and the rate of increase slowed down only slightly in the following decade. In 1963 the postwar 'bulge' generation began their higher education. A large proportion of a large generation shared the same collective conditions and experiences. Within the student population a substantial minority developed a radical consciousness, becoming what Mannheim would have referred to as a radical 'generational unit'.

A second factor to consider is the social origin of the activists. The common sense of identity of the radicals was partly a product of the permissive, liberal, middle-class backgrounds that many of them came from. Given the small number of socialists in the United States, a relatively large number of radicals had parents who held socialist beliefs. Many of the activists took seriously and tried to put into practice the progressive values of their parents. They felt that there was a huge gap between how society was and how they had been taught it ought to be. This feeling is apparent in the preamble to the Port Huron Statement of 1962 drawn up by the American radical group, Students for a Democratic Society (SDS): 'We are people of this generation, bred in at least modest comfort, housed now in universities, looking uncomfortably to the world we inherit' (Jacobs and Landau 1967: 155).

Third, any account of an historical movement must recognize that the meanings the actors themselves give to their actions are causes in the chain of events. Certain issues worried the young radicals and they set out to do something about them. To quote the Port Huron Statement again:

'As we grew, however, our comfort was penetrated by events too troubling to dismiss. First, the permeating and victimizing fact of human degradation, symbolized by the southern struggle against racial bigotry, compelled most of us from silence to activism. Second, the enclosing fact of the Cold War.'   (Jacobs and Landau 1967: 155)

For British activists the nuclear bomb was the major issue of the early 1960s, and in the mid-1960s the Vietnam War was internationally regarded as the main cause for concern. By the end of the decade the nature of international capitalism itself had become the central consideration. Marxism was strong among prominent European student activists throughout the decade, but it was not until the late 1960s that even a significant minority of American students adopted Marxist analysis.

A matter that troubled the radicals throughout the 1960s was what they saw and experienced as the alienating nature of modern, bureaucratic society. Some of them perceived university life in this way, and they expected no better from careers in large government or business organizations. They consistently argued for more personal and democratic participation in decision-making – in all organizations. The term *participatory democracy* was used to describe this approach. In a similar spirit, they attempted to revive the ideal of community which they felt was being swamped by the values of functional efficiency and profit. Some went so far as to 'drop out' and join the commune movement, but many worked for their ideals within existing organizations and, a little older now, may still be doing so.

The above factors do not occur separately. The responses people make (the third factor, above) to the social and political situation always to some extent reflect their immediate social environment (second factor, above). Writing of the American radicals, Charles Hampden-Turner draws these points together by contrasting the humanistic ideals experienced by the radicals in their early upbringing with the far tougher world of commerce and politics ahead of them:

'It has long seemed to me only a matter of time before the developmental (and humanistic) themes in American life confronted the repressive themes, and before those students nurtured in the better homes and schools came to regard the opportunities offered by business and government as an insult to their achieved levels of psycho-social development.'
(Hampden-Turner 1971: 419–20)

A difference between the United States and British student movements needs to be noted. The former was predominantly idealistic and liberal in ideology and practice, whereas the latter contained a strong element of socialism in addition. Simply, this difference reflects a wider difference in the social life and political traditions of the two countries.

A final factor must be noted in explaining the causation of the movement – the influence of the media. The general processes analysed by Stanley Cohen and Dick Hebdige in relation to the media and British youth subcultures also occurred in the United States (see Chapter 3). The concept of amplification used by Cohen seems applicable to several 'outbreaks' of protest during the history of the movement. Support for the sit-ins against segregation in the early 1960s certainly increased after media coverage. In 1968 media amplification of the student 'revolt' seemed to occur on a global scale, with major events happening in New York, Chicago, Paris, London, and elsewhere. The media rarely, if ever, causes outbreaks of student protest or subcultural events, but it can influence their course, size, and duration.

Hebdige's point that youth subcultures are areas of contest between some of their more creative members and commercial and media interests is as applicable to the United States as to Britain. Some of the radicals attempted to 'subvert' the media by using it to popularize their own causes. The political-cultural radicals, the Yippies, did this most spectacularly if, sometimes, to obscure purpose. Two Yippies, Jerry Rubin and Abbie Hoffman, were tried along with several other radicals on conspiracy charges in Chicago following the alternative convention of 1968. They attempted to use the courtroom as a stage on which to dramatize their views. Among other ploys, they dressed up as national figures in order to ridicule the 'system' and its leading representatives. Phil Ochs, a protest singer who was tried along with Rubin and Hoffman, describes their philosophy:

'The idea of the Yippie was to be a form of theatre politics, theatrically dealing with what seemed to be an increasingly absurd world and trying to deal with it on other than a straight moral level. They wanted to be able to act out fantasies ... and communicate their feeling to the public.'

(in Claver and Spitzer 1970: 287)

As the following remark by Abbie Hoffman indicates, philosophy is perhaps too strong a word to describe the Yippies' outlook: 'We didn't have any particular kind of program that we were bringing to Chicago, but we were bringing a kind of life style' (in Claver and Spitzer 1970: 352).

Activities

1 Find out what you can about the widespread fear of communism in the United States in the 1950s, as it showed itself in domestic affairs.

2 The American student movement originally adopted a strategy of non-violent change. Discuss why you think a minority turned to a strategy of violent revolutionary change in the late 1960s.

3 Which parts of the quotation from Charles Hampden-Turner refer to the general factors discussed in the text?

What kind of movement was it? Some views and models

Before presenting a number of sociological perspectives and models on the movement, it is important to bear in mind some differences between the political and cultural wings. Initially, the political wing was a loosely linked body of like-minded pressure groups. Most activists were deeply opposed to totalitarian communism but wanted to achieve more radical solutions than those offered by mainstream liberalism. Many moved through a radical phase back into the system, a few became Marxists, but a number did attempt to work out and implement their ideals more originally. It is this group, which went 'the whole way', that we shall discuss below. The cultural wing was similarly diffuse and diverse. For many the counter-culture or the 'politics of life style' soon faded into adulthood without setting them seriously against 'the system'. Again, however, there were a few who did strive to create an alternative life style. It is the cultural and political 'core' movement that we mainly have in mind below.

Unsurprisingly, the major critique of the new radicals in the United States came from those liberal academics who had often been their target. In *The Politics of Unreason* (1971), Seymour M. Lipset and Earl Raab frankly compared the new radicalism of the left with the American right. They suggest a typology of 'extremism' applicable to the 'far' right and left, arguing that extremist movements share the following charac-teristics: simplism, moralism, populism (a back to the people impulse), and a tendency to indulge in conspiratorial theory. A movement characterized by these traits is referred to as 'monistic' – its members believe that they alone are right (moralism) and attribute low motives to those who disagree with them (conspiratorial theory).

In a similar vein, several liberal academics used Freudian concepts to demonstrate the irrationality and intolerance of the new radicalism. Robert Nisbet (1970), for instance, argued that the student activists were so determined to experience the satisfaction, security, and love of community that they ignored the practical requirement of emotional control and organizational restraint. Or, in Freudian terms, they embraced the pleasure principle but rejected the reality principle. Edward Shils (1969) contended that the activists had not learnt the limits of scarcity: that in material, emotional, or even moral terms it is not possible to have everything one wants. In size, at least, Lewis Feuer's *The Conflict of Generations* (1969) was the major interpretation of the new radicalism from a liberal. Basing his thesis on Freud's concept of the oedipal complex, Feuer maintains that there is a natural conflict between father and son (i.e. between the generations), the youthful energy for which is normally diverted into work. However, students are not disciplined by

107

labour and oedipal energy is prone to take its original, primitive form. Thus student 'rebellions'.

The essential liberal-Freudian criticism that the student movement sometimes lacked realism, amounting even to emotional self-indulgence, has an element of truth in it. However, the liberal academics scarcely recognize the positive and creative elements in the youthful idealism. For a balanced assessment of the activists' radical idealism, Hampden-Turner's (1971) views and Marcuse's comments (see p. 109) also need to be considered.

The new radicalism was not predominantly socialist or Marxist, and has been criticized by socialist thinkers. While welcoming the radical impulses and sentiments of the activists, Tom Bottomore (1967) takes the view that they lacked both the coherent ideology and organization to become a permanent 'new' force. For him, socialism remains the only alternative to capitalism and (writing in the mid-1960s) he hoped that the new radicals would turn in that direction. Christopher Lasch (1970) argues that 'the agony of the American Left' has been caused precisely by the lack of a socialist party with mass appeal in the United States. As a result, radicalism in America has been a cultural phenomenon, confined to the realm of ideas and, he virtually implies, wishful-thinking.

Both liberal and Marxist critiques of the new radicalism find a lack of ideological and organizational realism. Hall and Jefferson add the interesting idea that the new radicalism, particularly the counterculture, was part of a wider cultural adaptation to the postwar expansion of the capitalist consumer market and in this way was functional to capitalism:

> 'Advanced capitalism now required, not thrift but consumption; not sobriety but style; not postponed gratifications but immediate satisfaction of needs; not goods that last but things that are expendable: the "swinging" rather than the sober life style.'   (Hall and Jefferson 1976: 64)

They go on to quote Irwin Silber:

'"One of the main functions of radical upheavals ... is to engender the new ideas, techniques, attitudes, and values which a developing society requires but which the proprietors of its superstructure are unable to bring into being themselves because their social position is inevitably tied to the status quo."'

However, Hall and Jefferson do recognize that 'authentic countercultural values' and 'focal concerns (such as more communal living arrangements)' did emerge. They accept Marcuse's view that these new concerns and forms may 'prefigure' aspects of what a genuinely liberated society might be like. However, they see the working class as the primary agency of liberation, not the mainly middle-class radicals. This noticeably modifies their enthusiasm for the new radicalism. While accepting that the 'radical transformation of a social system still depends on the class which constitutes the human base of the process of production' (i.e. the working class), Marcuse found that it was the 'young rebels' who were actually making a break with capitalism, albeit only at the cultural level, and even there only partially and insecurely. Otherwise, he perceived a pervasive 'one-dimensional' conformity in American society, not least among the working class (Marcuse 1969a/b).

The recurrent criticism in the above views of the movement is of its lack of realism. However, none of them satisfactorily develop an adequate typology. Lipset's and Raab's terminology (simplism rather than simple, moralism rather than moral) is frankly too biased for their description of it as a 'monistic' movement to be accepted. In my view, the more familiar term 'idealistic movement' is preciser. As used here, idealism refers to a commitment to implement values perceived as fundamental, with little or no compromise. By contrast, liberalism centrally accepts compromise as realistically necessary. Marxism also 'realistically' considers that socialist values can only be achieved if material conditions and political possibilities allow it. Idealism is therefore a distinct political and cultural form, though it usually occurs in the form of occasional romantic movements rather than in a stable organization, such as a political party. An historical parallel to the new radicalism, on a smaller scale, was perhaps the cultural-political radicalism of the youthful Wordsworth, Coleridge, Southey, and others in the post-French Revolution fervour. At one point they discussed returning 'to nature' by establishing a commune on the Susquehanna river in the United States. More recently, the bohemians of Greenwich Village in New York in the 1920s, and the 1950s beatniks of the West Coast were romantic precursors of the 1960s radicals. Idealistic or romantic movements tend to be emotional, morally idealistic, espouse communal ideals, produce charismatic leaders, and adopt naturalistic or primitivist attitudes and behaviour (a comparison between hippie and American Indian style and behaviour might illustrate the last point). Norman Cohn's observation on millenarian religious movements – that unless they become institutionalized they go through a cycle of rapid growth and decline – is applicable to all idealistic movements, including that of the 1960s.

Marcuse's insight (1969a/b) that the new radicalism may have prefigured emerging forms of social life can be used crucially to qualify the categorization of it as an idealistic movement. As Marcuse was aware, the conversion of work-time into leisure-time by the means of new technology has the potential to liberate human beings on a mass scale. 'Ideal' (in the sense of more fulfilling and liberated) life styles would be possible on a general rather than simply an elite basis, if existing material and cultural resources were distributed to achieve this. Currently, in Britain and the United States, there has been a reaction against the 'permissive sixties' and a reassertion of the 'need' for hard work. However, it may yet be that the 1960s radicals' vision of the future was as 'realistic' as that offered by the ideology of Thatcherism and Reaganism. We return to this issue in Chapter 6.

Activities

1 Describe and explain some of the ways in which the radicals of the early 1960s felt alienated.

2 Consider whether the concept of alienation is of any use in describing your personal feelings about aspects of your own life.

3 Critically discuss Marcuse's notion that the new radicalism may have 'prefigured' in certain ways what a liberated society might be like.

Further reading

The radicalism of the 1960s is too remote to be considered contemporary and too recent to be regarded as history. Consequently there are relatively few measured assessments of it. The best way to study the movement is probably through the various collections of articles and documents published about it during the 1960s and early 1970s. These include Jacobs and Landau (eds) (1967), and Teodori (1970). Hall's and Jefferson's opening essay in Resistance through Rituals *(1976) contains a section on the new radicalism. For those who want to grapple with them, Marcuse's works are still widely available. His Political Preface (1966) to* Eros and Civilization *(1969a) and* An Essay in Liberation *(1969b) are the most relevant here.*

There are two books which give a real feel of the 'spirit of the sixties' which I have not mentioned in the text. They are Roszak (1973), and Reich (1970). Most large libraries should have them. Broadly, these books reflect the more optimistic side of Marcuse but are far more accessible than his writings. Crick and Robson (1970) contains articles covering the student movement internationally, including Britain.

Finally, if your teacher or lecturer is between thirty-five and forty-five and occasionally looks like a faded hippie, you may find him or her worth interviewing about the 1960s!

6

A future for youth?

I cannot imagine writing a book on age and generation without attempting to confront the problems facing contemporary youth. I have spent most of my working life teaching 16–19 year olds and feel a particular involvement with them. I trust this subjective concern will inform rather than distort what follows.

Nobody could have predicted the massive and virtually continuous rise in unemployment from the mid-1970s to well over three million in 1984. Coming onto a glutted labour market, young people were particularly hard hit by unemployment. By early 1984, 40 per cent of Britain's unemployed were under 25 and a third of these had been unemployed for over a year. The estimated unemployment figure for 16–19 year olds was over 800,000. While the majority of young people still get jobs on leaving full-time education, the overshadowing possibility of unemployment has affected the thinking and attitudes of a generation. Responses vary across the spectrum. Some react by working prodigiously hard for qualifications and zealously conforming to the requirements, real or imagined, of teachers or employers, in the hope that a good reference or a job will be the reward. Arguably, this is a rational response to a cruelly competitive situation. Others, when they sense academic failure in the offing or experience rejection in the labour market, get angry and bitter. But there is no firm evidence that the young of the 1980s are particularly radical. Rather, they produce a variety of responses and 'solutions' to the dilemmas presented by the educational system and the state of the labour market.

The relationship between education and the economy is the focus of this brief chapter but, as we shall see, this matter stimulates crucial wider considerations about the future of our society and of the young within it.

Education and (un)employment policies so far

Government response to the early rise in youth unemployment was swift. In 1975 the Job Creation Projects (JCPs), which Kenneth Roberts calls 'the direct ancestors of the YTS', were launched. Although not allowed to compete with commercial enterprises or do work that would otherwise be done by public services, the JCPs did carry out some projects from which communities benefited. However, youth unemployment continued to rise and it became clear that young people had specific training and work experience needs. In 1976 the Work Experience Programme (WEP) for 16–18 year olds was established. In 1978 the Manpower Services Commission (MSC) initiated the Youth Opportunities Programme (YOP), to rationalize and oversee provisions for unemployed youth. A variety of state-subsidized work experience was offered.

Over 80 per cent of the *initial* YOP trainees got jobs within eight months of entering the programme, but the YOP initiative was undercut by the continued rapid expansion of youth unemployment. By 1982 YOP was handling 550,000 trainees, well over twice the number originally envisaged. Most of these returned to unemployment after completing their programme.

As YOP faltered other policies were introduced, but the government's main effort was a New Training Initiative announced in 1981. The major aspect of this was to be the Youth Training Scheme (YTS). YTS is comprehensive in that it offers to *all* 16 year olds who would otherwise be unemployed some further education and preparation for work. In the longer term, the government aims for at least one year's training for all 16-year-old school leavers.

The major left-wing criticism of YTS and most other MSC-administered schemes is that they are in reality exercises in the social control of a redundant group which masquerade as training programmes. Denis Gleeson puts the point sharply:

> 'The push towards training reform may have little to do with equipping labour with specific technical skills to make it more employable, but perhaps more to do with establishing "substitute criteria" (vocational preparation, work experience, further education, and so forth) for controlling the aspirations of disaffected young people.'

(Gleeson 1983: 1)

Without offering a detailed critique of YTS and other government initiatives, which apparently seek to link the educational system more closely with the world of work, I would like to suggest that the policy initiatives from 1975 have been conceived in too narrow and piecemeal a way. This may have been historically inevitable, given the unpredicted extent of youth unemployment, but there is no need to persist in these attitudes. There are other ways of envisaging the future of youth than that implied by these policies, and I shall consider some of them now. I shall also argue that the future of youth is often not very distinct from the future of others.

Futures for youth

In the following discussion, I shall draw substantially on two books: Kenneth Roberts, *School Leavers and Their Prospects: Youth and the Labour Market in the 1980s* (1984), and A.G. Watts, *Education, Unemployment and the Future of Work* (1983). What I refer to as 'futures for youth', Roberts terms 'alternatives', and Watts 'scenarios'. Some of the suggestions below are mutually exclusive but others would be most effective in combination. Although concerned with a much wider group, Watts's suggestions have a particular applicability to youth.

Unemployment

The scenario of high unemployment is what we have now and only the perverse would wish to recommend it. The major evil of a continued high level of long-term unemployment especially is that it is socially divisive. It creates two nations even more than the traditional class system does. This is because the groups particularly at risk from unemployment – the young, the old, women, the disabled, the unskilled, and ethnic minorities – have little other than unemployment in common and are poorly placed to act collectively. High unemployment creates a nation of 'haves' and 'have nots', and the young are disproportionately among the latter. A particular danger for the young unemployed is that their self-respect is damaged and their transition to adulthood impeded.

Leisure

It is arguable that technological advance has made possible the creation of a new leisure class. For the 'unemployed' to become a leisure class would require that others perceive and treat them differently than now. Thus it would become accepted as normal that many do not work. In order to live at an acceptable level members of the leisure class would need a guaranteed minimum income, and perhaps free access to a range of services and resources.

Neither Roberts nor Watts believe that this alternative is an adequate way of dealing with (youth) unemployment. Watts

115

argues that employment has elements of necessity and reciprocity (involving exchange with others) missing in leisure activity. Leisure activity alone does not sufficiently bind a person to society or give him/her identity. Roberts bluntly dismisses leisure solutions as 'unnecessary and unworkable'. He argues that human needs can generate work indefinitely, and that technological advance does not so much replace people as release them to do other work.

My own view is that the long-term decline of hours in employment and the corresponding increase in leisure will continue. If so, how this extra 'free' time will be shared between groups and how the more leisured groups will acquire income are problems that need to be considered. The changes in attitude required are so profound that many would find an abrupt change to a leisure society acutely disruptive. However, in principle, a further shift in that direction may be desirable.

Training and education

As Roberts points out, there are few principled objections to more and better training. However, he does raise the question of whether blanket schemes are the best approach, and he reminds us of the need to fund training for specific jobs as well as 'transferable' skills. The debate about how improved training might be achieved cannot be pursued here, but it is worth noting that Britain commits much fewer resources to the training of 16–18 year olds than several other major western European countries.

On the matter of education, Roberts is particularly interesting. He argues that the separation of students that takes place at sixteen plus into an academic track (mainly 'A' levels) and a vocational track (largely academic 'failures') means that the latter has a built-in lower status. The solution is to make sixteen plus education genuinely comprehensive. The need is not for large doses of vocationalism for the less academic, but equality of status for vocational or work-related courses for all:

'The main structural reform required to unblock British education's mainstream is the public examination at 16 plus. These exams were designed to weed out all but a talented few. It is inevitable that the majority fail and are left with nowhere to travel up the educational ladder. As Wilby (1979) argues, the main problem with Britain's comprehensives is that their standards are artificially high rather than too low. The most radical proposals for opening opportunities at 16 plus would abolish public examination at this age and design curricula on the assumption that young people will remain in education until age 17 or 18. Other proposals would merge 'O' levels and CSEs, then replace 'A' levels with an examination within the majority's capacities. Sweden and the USA have broad-based mainstreams that encourage all young people to remain in full-time education at least until age 18. Having opened the mainstream it will be possible to inject some of the relevance that the vocational track's supporters seek by revising traditional notions of ability, rewriting curricula, and ceasing to treat the abstract as more worthy than the applicable.' (Roberts 1984: 97)

I would add that many courses for sixteen plus would acquire greater interest and relevance simply by being opened to adults. It might help to clarify thinking if we did not conceive of education as either *for* work or *instead of* work, but for creative, skilful activity of any kind. Often the new vocational emphasis fails to do this, with potentially disastrous results. Those who imagine they are using vocationalism or prevocationalism to prepare students for the whole of life are likely to delude themselves as well as the students, and may end up as 'soft cops' for policing the unemployed. Work orientation and vocational preparation have their place within education, but they are not the basis of it. Education is about realizing human potential, and we stray from that principle at the risk of authoritarianism, more or less.

Employment and work

Watts makes a very important distinction between employment and work. He suggests that employment is 'paid work' in the formal economy and is often, quite misleadingly, thought of as work itself. He uses the term work to include self-employment and work in three informal economies – the black economy, the communal economy (e.g. charitable work), and the household economy. He refers to this as the 'free economy', as distinct from the 'institutional economy'. This distinction has the merit of opening up the way we conceive of productive activity in the future.

Both Watts and Roberts favour policies to achieve higher employment as conventionally understood. They approve of strong government initiatives to stimulate the economy and generate employment, rather than relying on the revival of private enterprise as the Thatcher administrations have done. They both subscribe to a 'right to work' philosophy and discuss sympathetically such ideas as a shorter working week and job-sharing to help achieve it.

In a stimulating chapter entitled 'The Work Scenario', Watts attempts to suggest ways in which the 'free economy' might acquire comparable rewards and status with the 'institutional economy'. He argues that in part the black economy exists because to declare income would prevent some people from obtaining benefits. He suggests a negative income tax system which would take little, if any, of what was declared away from the less well-off. He also proposes that 'Ways should be found of measuring – and thereby attaching value to – work within the household and communal economies.' A basic level of reward for this work could be secured by a national minimum income policy. One effect of this would be radically to improve the situation of what has traditionally been regarded as 'women's work'. If work in the house and community were securely rewarded with more money, status, and power, perhaps many more young men would be attracted to these areas. In any case, such innovation might open up a range of possibilities for all young people of a kind that now we can only strain to imagine.

1970s commentators on the 1980s: Phil Cohen and Paul Willis
Interestingly, two influential commentators on working-class

youth subcultures, Phil Cohen and Paul Willis, have published articles on youth (again, mainly working-class youth) in the 1980s.

Cohen's two articles, 'School for Dole' (1982) and 'Losing the Generation Game' (1984), are overtly political and appeared in *New Socialist*. Perhaps because they were written at the height of Margaret Thatcher's success, they are rather sombre in tone. If there was some reluctance to accept the decline and break-up of the traditional working class in the work of the Centre for Cultural Studies in the 1970s, Cohen now feels that fragmentation applies as equally to working-class youth as to adult culture. He still sees residual signs of working-class masculinity and aggression within the subcultures, but accepts that many better-off working-class 'kids' are seduced by consumerism and are far from revolutionary. Apart from the better off, 'not only the unskilled, the unorganized, and the unemployed, but young people who would previously have grown up socialists' are attracted by 'the glittering array of youth cultures'. Yet Cohen sees no point in reiterating the socialist message to youth in the old way. They have already shown their lack of interest. The young now 'talk a different language' – that of the subcultures. He believes that for a political party to communicate effectively with youth, it will have to learn the 'codes' of youth. So far the dialogue has barely begun (though perhaps Neil Kinnock's celebrated video with Tracey Ullman was a start?).

In early 1984, Paul Willis published three articles in *New Society*: 'Youth Unemployment: 1 A New Social State', 'Youth Unemployment: 2 Ways of Living', and 'The Land of Juventus' (an imagined description of a kind of 'youthtopia'). He describes the articles as 'speculative rather than ethnographic'. In the first, he makes the point that for many working-class young a radical change has occurred: the transition to full adult identity through work is no longer securely available. Instead they are offered 'dependency' – on the state and, often, on their parents. In his second article he presents a variety of responses to this 'new social state'. Some young males respond bitterly and angrily, others appear to accept a decline of the traditional male 'breadwinning' role. One response among girls is to opt for early pregnancy and the tough independence of a single-parent home. He then examines what it is like to be workless in a consumer society. A key description of the young unemployed is that they are 'consumers without consumer power' – just as dazzled as the employed by the high street display but unable to buy – except by the niggardly indulgence of the welfare state.

It is in his third article that Willis gets into top speculative gear. In Juventus all young people over sixteen are guaranteed a 'wage' of about half that of the average industrial worker. There is also a Youth Guarantee, by which the state agrees to commit enough resources to young people to enable them to participate in productive or otherwise meaningful activity. This includes the support of an 'alternative sector', involving co-operatives, voluntary organizations, community groups, and community workshops. Some older housing stock is handed over to young people to form housing co-operatives, and local authorities and voluntary organizations adopt 'open space' and 'free resource' policies in respect of a range of materials and equipment. Recognizing that the 'kids' have moved from the back streets to the high streets, Willis suggests that the latter be made into attractive places in which to meet and spend time rather than left merely as commercial bazaars. The leisurely, open squares of some older Italian towns occurred to me as a relevant model, or perhaps the new Covent Garden is close to the mark.

In an interesting reference. Willis returns to a concern with style typical of the subcultural analysis of the 1970s. In Juventus the young have the upper hand in the battle with the forces of commerce:

'In the old days, some young people carried out parasitic style-wars, based on ready-made fashion and youth consciousness industries. They took the fashions on offer, but rearranged them into a whole series of youth styles. Now many more groups of young people produce styles and fashions locally, and produce and play their own music locally. These are becoming a means of genuinely personal and small-group artistic expression.'   (Willis 1984c: 58–9)

It is all very stimulating. There is nothing in the spirit of what Willis writes which is incompatible with the more conventionally phrased suggestions of Roberts and Watts. However, what young people get will depend partly on what they themselves demand.

Activities

1 Critically evaluate the 'futures for youth' suggested in this chapter.

2 How do you envisage the young and old relating in future society? (See Chapter 7 for information on the old.)

Further reading

Current publications of all sorts are the best source for this topic. Newspapers, The Times Educational Supplement, New Society *and weeklies or monthlies with a more general circulation frequently carry articles on contemporary youth. It is simply a question of keeping an eye open for them.*

Anyone at all interested in this area will find the books by Watts (1983) and Roberts (1984) that were discussed in this chapter most useful. There are many worthwhile contributions in Gleeson (1983), particularly Horne's article, 'Youth Unemployment Programmes: An Historical Account of the Development of "Dole Colleges"' which is an interesting reminder that many 'contemporary' youth issues and policies were argued through in the 1930s.

7

Adulthood (young adults, the middle-aged, and the elderly)

Young adulthood and middle age

Although there is a growing body of research into the age 'stages' of young adulthood and middle age, particularly the latter, there is not yet a clear outline of 'a sociology of' these years. In modern society childhood, youth, and old age are relatively sharply differentiated and accordingly sociologists have been able to plot the ground.

The difference between these two age groupings and the others is that, for most, young adulthood and middle age are the productive years in the basic sense of having and rearing children, and making a living. These people are the workers on whom the dependent groups rely, directly or indirectly (through taxation). Most sociology is, in fact, about the crucial activities of these age groups, but this work largely takes age for granted. This is by no means illogical because class, gender, racial, and cultural variables are apparently more significant in these areas than the precise age of a mature adult. It is possible to hold almost any sort of job at any level at, say, 29 or 49.

It is notoriously difficult to stratify the adult years prior to old age. Dorothy Rogers (1972) points out that estimates of the span of middle age vary from 45–64 years to 30–70 years. I myself find that my students howl with incredulity when, following Erickson, I suggest that young adulthood might stretch to 40. Bernice Neutgarten (1974), a leading expert on age, suggests that 'age segregation is growing' in modern society, and certain behavioural norms do govern given age spans. Thus, a 50 year old trying to live it up in a teenage discotheque is recognizably failing to act his age. However, Neutgarten does not spell the normative structures out clearly, and the two age 'stages' under consideration remain ill defined.

In order to give focus to this discussion, I have decided to use Erickson's model of life-cycle stages (see *Table 2*). This is my fullest usage of Erickson's approach and provides an opportunity to cite some criticisms of it.

Young adulthood

Erickson states that the psycho-social crisis of young adulthood is 'intimacy versus isolation'. The related task is to achieve lasting relationships and career commitments, which seems an accurate description of the challenges most young adults face. Along the same lines, Dorothy Rogers writes of the 'merger self' and 'seeker self' of young adulthood. Early adulthood is less reflective than middle age, and is more concerned with the work of fashioning a base for both a personal and occupational future.

Two comments must be made on Erickson's conceptualization of early adulthood. First, his emphasis on individual development leads him to underestimate structural conflict. The experience of many young adults is largely defined by their place in organizational authority structures. Often this brings the young end of this age group particularly into a conflict of interests with the middle-aged, whose position and authority

123

they aspire to. This conflict is usually muted, because younger adults are often subordinate to older ones and dependent on them for advancement. There are countless exceptions to this, of course, but it is a dimension of generational conflict that could be explored further.

Second, Erickson insufficiently explores the effect of cultural and demographic variations throughout his stage-task model. I will take here the demographic factor, as it has so far been less explored in this book, and apply it particularly to young adults, although it is equally, if not more, relevant to adolescents. Two recent books written in the United States have argued that relative generational size is an important explanatory variable of generational experience. They are Richard A. Easterlin's *Birth and Fortune: The Impact of Numbers on Personal Welfare* (1980) and Ira Steinberg's *The New Lost Generation: The Problems of the Population Boom* (1982). Easterlin argues the general theory of population size effect more fully; his explanation of generational size is overwhelmingly economic. The postwar economic boom helped to generate the baby boom (in addition there was the effect of wartime restraint on producing children). The reduction in fertility rates in the 1960s and 1970s reflected the attempt of a large young adult generation to defend its standard of living in recessionary times by having fewer children. Thus they produced a smaller generation.

Steinberg examines the problems of the large birth cohorts of 1945–65 in the United States (with the exception of 1947–50) in more detail. Most western European countries, including Britain, had a similar immediate postwar baby boom, and a longer boom lasting up to about 1964 followed by a decline in annual births. Steinberg argues that the size of the 1945–65 group has exacerbated problems of employment. Those born in the early part of this period, who are now in their thirties, have run into problems of promotion and job mobility (both geographically in the same occupation and in seeking to change occupations). Steinberg quotes the teaching profession in the United States as an example of where these problems have occurred, and certainly the same is true of Britain. In both countries matters have been made much more difficult because of falling school rolls (the result of the decline in births after 1964–65). Teachers currently in their thirties, then, suffer a double demographic disadvantage. Their frustration and disillusionment, and that of others of their 'generation', is the key theme of Steinberg's book. Steinberg is particularly sensitive to the problems of women who have entered the labour market in force just when the gateways to upward occupational mobility are typically overcrowded.

It may seem inappropriate to choose demographic factors, which fit in poorly with the expansive, humanistic inspiration of Erickson's model, with which to criticize him. However, the realities of demographic (and socio-cultural) variation are precisely the kind he considers insufficiently. These provide the context in which the stage tasks are met, and may modify or perhaps even radically change some of the tasks and related 'crises' themselves.

Middle age

According to Erickson, in middle age (roughly forty to sixty), a person's central life task typically moves to concern with others – family, society, and future generations. The related crisis is the tension between generativity and self-absorption. At this stage, the individual has the power and experience to 'give something back', to guide and motivate others. Erickson's work was published before the modern feminist movement got under way, and he presumes too easily that what middle-aged males and females have to regenerate is traditional gender roles.

Most writers on middle age agree that it is a time for reassessment, for looking at what has been done and what might still be done. Charles Handy (1984) comments that it is tempting, in one's fifties, to pause and look back on what has been achieved but that we have to move on. Both Dorothy Rogers and Bernice Neutgarten state that awareness of personal mortality, and therefore of the use of remaining time, become of central importance in middle age. Rogers suggests that many start counting time 'backwards from death instead of forward from birth'. Neutgarten points out that because of the 'empty nest' syndrome, many middle-aged people do suddenly have 'more time'. She suggests an Erickson-like challenge with contrasting possible outcomes: mastery over the use of time, or capitulation to decline and mortality (what Charles Handy refers to as 'a life-sentence to endless television and gardening'). I doubt whether the reassessment and reorientation common in middle age is either biologically programmed or universal. It seems to be a product of the position of middle age in the life-span itself, which makes it an obvious time for self-assessment.

The crisis of middle age does seem to be more specific and prolonged than the crises Erickson associates with other life stages. The latter are generally challenges involving active struggle and outcome, whereas in middle age the crisis involves introspection and stocktaking – stopping and thinking. Sometimes, the crisis of middle age is a crisis as conventionally understood – a time of stress and near or actual breakdown. Daniel Levitson (1978) suggests that between forty and forty-five a person tends to measure up the 'dreams' s/he aspired to against the reality s/he has in fact achieved. Realization of the gap between the two can be painful and damaging to self-image. At a less elevated level, loss of youth can be stressful for some. There are gender differences here. A woman who has 'traded on her looks' obviously has particular problems. But male narcissism can suffer hard blows in middle age too, as Hepworth and Featherstone discuss in an amusing chapter, 'Resistance at Forty-eight – Old Age Brinkmanship', in their *Surviving Middle Age* (1982).

Conclusion

Although the above discussion is a 'dialogue with' rather than a presentation of Erickson's ideas, it will help briefly to summarize some criticisms of his model. First, given his tendency to universalize his model, he could usefully have strengthened its empirical basis (mainly case studies of men) and included a larger number of women in it. Second, various authors have queried Erickson's ordering of the stage tasks (could intimacy not precede identity?) and even their inevitability or desirability. Third, as much of this book has indicated, cultural and demographic factors affect the experience of age groups in a way and to an extent Erickson does not explore. In a survey involving 9,100 respondents, Lacy and Hendricks (1980) failed to find consistent support for Erickson's model. Yet Erickson's stage theory is so richly suggestive that even if it is not 'true', one feels that it ought to be. As La Rochefoucault said: 'One of the tragedies of life is the murder of a beautiful theory by a brutal gang of facts.'

Activities

1 Would you say that Erickson's model of psycho-social development is insufficiently sociological?

2 As young adulthood and middle age tend to be the 'forgotten ages' (taken for granted?), you might like to do some original research (interviews, questionnaires) into the subject.

Further reading

Two books I have not referred to directly in the text are well worth buying (and cheap!). They are: Fiske (1979) and Sheehy (1981). In general, popular literature in this area needs to be approached cautiously – it tends to be strong on generalization and weak on data.

Old age

The demographic imperative

Like most other western European countries, Britain has an ageing population. In 1911 the number of elderly people (women over 60 and men over 65) was 2.9 million, and in 1981 it was 9.8 million – an increase from 6.8 to 17.7 per cent of the population. However, the demographic trends between 1978 and 2011 for those aged 65–74 and those aged 75 plus are likely to be significantly different. The numbers of people between 65 and 74 is expected to fall because of Second World War casualties and the high rate of postwar emigration. By 1990, however, the numbers of people aged 75 and over is likely to increase by 500,000 to 3.5 million, and to go on increasing to 24 per cent above the 1978 figure. It is the 75 plus group that is most likely to become dependent; about 17 per cent of them currently need regular care of some kind. The 65–74 age group is much healthier, and is generally in a different life-situation from the very old. The huge increase in the dependent population of the elderly has attracted the concern both of government and social policy theorists. Such a change in population structure requires response on a different scale than in the past, both quantitatively – in terms of resources – and qualitatively – in terms of humanity and imagination.

The social construction of old age

A comparative perspective As we saw in the case of youth, comparative data help to establish what is open to cultural variation in social life and what seems to be universal. Donald Cowgill and Lowell Holmes and their colleagues (1972) made a comparative study of ageing in fourteen different societies, including preliterate, intermediate, and highly modern. Examples of each are, respectively, the Bantu society of Africa, Mexico, and the United States. On the basis of this research

128

they presented a number of 'universals', i.e. factors occurring in all the societies they studied, and a number of 'variations', i.e. factors varying significantly from society to society.

They present their findings in the form of propositions which they have tested, in some cases reformulated, and which they would like further tested. I have chosen to list from these propositions the five universals and ten variations that seem most significant to me:

Universals

1 In all societies, some people are classified as old and are treated differently because they are so classified.
2 There is a widespread tendency for people defined as old to shift to more sedentary, advisory, or supervisory roles involving less physical exertion and more concerned with group maintenance than with economic production.
3 In all societies, some old persons continue to act as political, judicial, and civic leaders.
4 In all societies, the mores prescribe some mutual responsibility between old people and their adult children.
5 All societies value life and seek to prolong it, even in old age.

Variations

1 Old age is identified in terms of chronological age chiefly in modern societies; in other societies onset of old age is more commonly linked with events such as a succession to eldership or becoming a grandparent.
2 Modernized societies have older populations, i.e. a higher proportion of old people.
3 The status of the aged is high in primitive societies, and is lower and more ambiguous in modern societies.
4 In primitive societies, older people tend to hold positions of political and economic power, but in modern societies such power is possessed by only a few.

5 The status of the aged is inversely proportional to the rate of social change.

6 The status of the aged tends to be high in agricultural societies and lower in urbanized societies.

7 Retirement is a modern invention; it is found chiefly in modern high-productivity societies.

8 The status of the aged is high in societies in which the extended form of the family is prevalent, and tends to be lower in societies which favour the nuclear form of the family and neolocal marriage.

9 With modernization the responsibility for the provision of economic security for the dependent aged tends to be shifted from the family to the state.

10 Disengagement (withdrawal from society) is not characteristic of the aged in primitive or agrarian societies, but an increasing tendency toward disengagement appears to accompany modernization.

There is only space to air some of the above propositions in the following pages. However, readers may find themselves stimulated to have their own discussion. A first point to note is the positivist methodology adopted by Cowgill and Holmes. They test their propositions about old age by the same comparative method that Eisenstadt used to test his hypotheses about age grades (see Chapter 1), except that they produce primary data whereas he relies on secondary. A second observation concerns Cowgill and Holmes's use of the term 'modernization'. They employ it to include advanced socialist as well as capitalist countries. While modernization theorists do argue a convergence between these two types of modern societies, as we shall see later when discussing old age in Britain, Marxists and radical sociologists tend to attribute the condition of the old in capitalist society to the nature of capitalism itself (see pp. 10–11 on Philip Abrams). They argue that, on the whole, the situation of the old is relatively better in socialist than in capitalist societies. In fairness, these more detailed considerations are not covered by the above propositions which are intentionally made at a very general level. Third, although Cowgill and Holmes find that the old have less status in modern than traditional, and in urban than rural societies they do not suggest that the level of family care and support has declined in the same way. The importance of this point will be more obvious after reading the next section.

An historical perspective   If the comparative work of Cowgill and Holmes tends to confirm widespread perceptions, that of Laslett and Wall on the history of ageing and the aged in England and Wales is rather more destructive of popular myth. The myth they expose is that the old were better treated in traditional England than now.

This view is itself partly based on another myth – that of the predominance of the extended family in pre-industrial England. In fact, Laslett and Wall show:

> '(T)he ordinary story of the family household after the child-rearing stage was of offspring leaving successively ... until, if the parents survived, they finally found themselves alone .... The wisps of evidence we have suggest that in some families elderly persons and children did live in close proximity, in others not.'

So the notion of a close-knit, caring extended family is undermined by the fact that this type of family system was much less common than has previously been thought. Laslett and Wall make what they call a 'telling contrast' with the traditional familial system of south China, where 'the rules of familial behaviour required co-residence wherever possible, and no father or mother of grown offspring would ever live alone'. They find further support for their view by examining family-related law in pre-industrial England, in which it is generally the immediate not the extended family that is held responsible for the care of the elderly. Finally, it should be noted that Laslett and Wall do not argue that England was typical of other pre-industrial societies in the above matters. They simply offer a single case-study.

131

Carole Haber's *Beyond Sixty-Five: the Dilemma of Old Ag*
in America's Past produces similar findings to Laslett and Wal
in one respect, for she also tends to conclude that there wa
never 'a golden age of senescence' in that country either
However, she emphasizes that the status of the elderly in th
United States probably declined during the nineteenth century
She does not explain this merely by reference to the relatec
processes of industrialization, urbanization, extended family
break-up, and the anomie of the old as modernization theorist:
tend to. Rather, she focuses in detail on the ways in which th
old became increasingly differentiated and marginalized from
the rest of society. Haber presents no grand theory, bu
recurrently describes situations in which other groups seek tc
impose their power and definitions on the old. The medical anc
social work professions played a significant part in this proces:
by repeatedly trying to categorize old age in terms of fixec
medical criteria. Had the medicalization of old age succeeded
these professions would have had a 'captive' clientèle tc
work on. Even as it is, there is a tendency in the United States tc
regard old age as an unfortunate if not quite a medica
condition.

Another factor which served to compartmentalize the olc
was the growth of occupational pension schemes by privat
employers. This both upstaged the trade unions and thei
demand for a universal state pension, and removed elderly
workers from the labour market. Similarly, the increasing
provision of charitable institutions for the elderly was in par
self-interest masquerading as philanthropy. Apart from tax
exemptions, this was a way of passing on 'the problem' of th
old to someone else. Haber concludes that, by the end of th
century, the status transition to retirement had become more
abrupt.

Laslett and Wall's historical work is complemented by more
contemporary studies of the family life of old people in
postwar Britain. If the traditional family is over-romanticized,
it seems that there has been a parallel tendency to underestimate the attention and care extended by the modern family to

132

its older members. Peter Townsend's study of the family life of the old in east London (1957) refuted the pessimists, discovering that the elderly were typically much involved with their children and grandchildren, from whom they received both emotional and practical support. Generalizing more widely, Richard Titmuss (1959) claimed that: 'The proportion of people aged over sixty-five accommodated in hospitals and institutions of all kinds is lower today than it was when the Royal Commission on the Poor Laws reported in 1909.' Figures given by Michael Anderson (1980) show that this was still the case in 1966: almost 6 per cent of the population aged sixty-five and over were living in Poor Law institutions in 1906; in 1966 1.9 per cent were living in homes for the aged, 1.7 per cent in hospitals and 0.9 per cent in psychiatric institutions, a total of 4.4 per cent. The comparable total for the United States was about 5 per cent.

One reason for these figures is that families are substantially wealthier now than they were at the turn of the century: they can afford to help their older kin more. Second, the old age pension (introduced after the Poor Law Commission reported) may be inadequate as a sole source of income, but it saves some elderly people from having to enter institutions. Thus many older people do seem to achieve virtual independence within the context of family interest and support.

Whether the family will be able to sustain its old quite so effectively in the future is open to conjecture. Three factors militate against it doing so. First, the substantial expected increase in the seventy-five and over age group, a larger proportion of which require intensive and expensive care. Second, a number of other demographic and social changes may weaken the kinship network as a source of care for the elderly by reducing the potential number of care-givers. These include the decline in the birth-rate, the tendency to defer parenthood, the increase in divorce and one-parent families, and the increase in the number of women in the labour market. This last development is crucial for although we speak of 'family care', in fact this usually means female and, specifically, daughter care of the old. Third, even if their capacity to give care were not reduced by increased labour-market activity, the ideology of women's liberation may lead many women to question whether this 'labour of love' should fall to them so often.

Marxist and socialist perspectives Chris Phillipson's *Capitalism and the Construction of Old Age* is written from a committed socialist perspective. He argues strongly that old age in capitalist society is structured by capitalism itself. He summarizes his own arguments as follows:

'The experience of growing old must be viewed as an event heavily influenced by class and gender relations; to view it as a period where the biological process of age assumes a primary role is to ignore the cumulative power and significance of life in a class society; similarly, the form which experiences in retirement take (tensions in transition from work to retirement; poverty in old age) are not a consequence of individual characteristics or the process of ageing, but reflect the influence of numerous forms of inequality within capitalism; ideologies of retirement and the care of the elderly within homes and hospitals thus become examples of the way in which growing old is constructed through a range of policies imposed upon the older population.'   (Phillipson 1982: 167–68)

I shall return to policy issues later. Immediately, I will present the four reasons Phillipson gives for arguing that capitalism 'is irreconcilable with meeting the needs of elderly people':

1 Whenever capitalism is in crisis working people, particularly those who become unemployed and/or are forced into retirement, suffer most.
2 In capitalist society profits, law and order, and defence have priority over individual and social needs. Thus, in the first Thatcher administration, defence spending increased as a percentage of Gross Domestic Product while expenditure on social services was cut back.

3 Because of industrial decline in given areas, facilities can also decline rapidly and this 'can have a disastrous impact on the lives of elderly people'.
4 Capitalism remains a system of labour exploitation, and when the older worker leaves the wage system he or she is likely to experience a severe drop in income. The state pension is about half the average take-home pay of an industrial worker, yet for over 70 per cent of older people it is their main source of income.

Clearly, Phillipson is locating the problems faced by old people within the experience of the working class in capitalist society. He argues that the older worker has been gradually removed from the labour market in favour of supposedly more efficient or cheaper (often female) workers. In the immediate postwar period of expansion there was demand for the labour of older workers, but the 'crisis' of the early 1980s meant the position of the older worker 'changed dramatically' and s/he became virtually redundant to the needs of the system. At this point, Phillipson's argument seems identical to that of Peter Townsend, who claims that 'the dependency of the elderly in the twentieth century is being manufactured socially' (see p. 141).

Phillipson comments usefully on the varying experiences of men and women in retirement and old age. He notes how much better prepared, both materially and in terms of education, middle-class men are than working-class men to take an active rather than a passive attitude to retirement. He finds a growing contradiction between the new possibilities provided by expanding education and leisure opportunities, and the fragmented and alienating nature of manual work in modern capitalist society. Many working-class men are simply not prepared for retirement. In dealing with women, Phillipson distinguishes between those who have been concerned solely with domestic labour and those also involved in wage labour. Surveys suggest that the latter were often more resistant than men to retirement. He explains this by citing Jacobsohn's concept of 'anticipatory widowhood'. The (semi-skilled) women in Jacobsohn's sample looked ahead apprehensively to the isolation likely to follow the death of their husbands, and expressed greater attachment than men to relationships formed at work. Despite this, working-class women were more likely than middle-class women to retire simply to be with their retiring husbands. For women involved solely in domestic labour, a husband's retirement may bring an end to isolation. Equally, it may increase the 'caring' load, especially if he loses his health. Some women also experience a sense of losing their own 'territory' on the retirement of their husbands. Finally Phillipson stresses that, for the very old, issues of ill-health and loneliness are much more likely to arise.

Two comments can be made on Phillipson's work. First, as he freely accepts, he is unable to show that in Russia, the most advanced socialist society, the condition of the elderly is significantly better than in Britain. Indeed, he questions the validity of Russian socialism and, in the end, argues for a better deal for the old in terms of his own socialist principles. Second, useful though his class analysis of age is, there remains room for analysis of the general problems of age such as those of relative status decline, loneliness, and the need to prepare for death.

Activities

1 **In the light of other material so far presented in this chapter, critically discuss Cowgill and Holmes's 'universals' and 'variations' of old age.**

2 **Devise and conduct your own piece of research on old age. (Use the Harris research as a 'model' if necessary: see p. 138 in the next section.)**

Ageism, stigma, and stereotypes

Jon Hendricks and C. Davis Hendricks describe ageism very well:

'Gerontologists [researchers into old age] have coined the term ageism to refer to the pejorative image of someone who is old simply because of his or her age. Like racism or sexism, it is wholesale discrimination against all members of a category, though usually it appears in more covert form. Threatened cutbacks in social security, failure to provide meaningful outlets or activities, or the belief that those in their sixties or beyond do not benefit from psychotherapy are all examples of subtle, or in some cases not so subtle, appraisals of the old. Part of the myth, a fundamental if implicit element of ageism, is the view that the elderly are somehow different from our present and future selves and therefore not subject to the same desires, concerns, or fears.'

(Hendricks and Hendricks 1977: 14)

To view the old as 'somehow different from ourselves' is to dehumanize them. Hendricks and Hendricks's comments accord very well with Erving Goffman's concept of 'stigma'. To stigmatize an individual or group is to regard them as 'not quite human'. Thus to order a drink over the head of an old person, who has been waiting at the bar longer than you, is to treat them as a little less than human. Perhaps to classify 'old age' under the title of 'social problems', as one textbook does, is also to downgrade the elderly inadvertently. In modern European and American society, where the labour of the old is not required nor their wisdom much sought, they suffer the daily possibility of being patronized. We can probably all furnish examples from our own lives – *if* we care to think about it.

A stereotype is an oversimplified belief which tends to persist despite contradictory factual evidence. *Table 8* shows a high level of negative stereotypes about old age among the American public. The survey was carried out by the Harris polling organization for the National Council on the Ageing. Over 4,250 interviews were held with a representative cross-section of the public, including the elderly (sixty-five and over).

Clearly, many old people find old age less problematic than younger people expect. For every *one* elderly person who found

137

Table 8 *Differences between personal experiences of Americans aged 65 and over, and expectations held by other adults about those experiences*

	very serious problems experienced by the elderly themselves (percentage)	very serious problems the public expects the elderly to experience (percentage)	net difference
fear of crime	23	50	+27
poor health	21	51	+30
not having enough money to live on	15	62	+47
loneliness	12	60	+48
not having enough medical care	10	44	+34
not having enough education	8	20	+12
not feeling needed	7	54	+47
not having enough to do to keep busy	6	37	+31
not having enough friends	5	28	+23
not having enough job opportunities	5	45	+40
poor housing	4	35	+31
not having enough clothes	3	16	+13

things worse than expected, *three* found them better. Hendricks and Hendricks comment that on the whole: 'Income and racial background have been identified as having a greater impact on life satisfaction than does age.' Generally, the more affluent respondents were more satisfied with their life situation.

This last point is important. The old are stratified in social-class terms as are other age groups. For a substantial minority of the old in the United States, and perhaps a larger one in Britain, their 'problems' are caused by poverty rather than age. In these two societies most old people are 'marginalized', but it is those who then find themselves without adequate resources that experience deprivation. The broadly interactionist material referred to above does not suggest that the old do not have 'real' problems. Rather, by stripping away the myths and stereotypes we can see more clearly what those problems are. One of them, of course, is the existence of the stereotypes themselves.

Old age, politics, and social policy

The first part of this section will deal with issues affecting the minority of elderly people who need some kind of care and who are not able to live fully independently. The second part will examine policy perspectives and issues affecting the age group as a whole.

Care of the elderly

Elderly people in need of care rely on the family/community, government, or private enterprise, either separately or in combination. Historically, no political party can lay exclusive claim to being 'the party of the family' in the area of care policy. Mindful, perhaps, of the increasing burden of aged dependency, both the Labour and Conservative Parties have recently argued the merits of community care. In the late 1960s and early 1970s efforts were made to keep the needy old in the community by providing home helps, day-care centres, and other forms of assistance. In the late 1970s and early 1980s, family and voluntary help – sometimes referred to as 'the good neighbour policy' – were stressed. This approach was promoted by the Thatcher government but was strongly criticized for both its motives and methods by the Labour Party. The Conservative government facilitated the placement of old people in privately run homes for the aged by enabling their fees to be paid from public funds, and it also supported the work of such charities as Age Concern and Help the Aged.

The major criticism of the government's 'community care' policy was that it was an excuse for cost cutting. Faced with reduced resources from central government, local authorities were forced to provide first for the old who lived alone, leaving the family to look after its own dependent relatives. The jibe was that this was 'care on the cheap'. The danger was that in some cases it was no care at all. A second criticism is related to the first. The burden of care falls disproportionately on women. According to an Equal Opportunities Commission Survey (1978; see Phillipson 1982), three times as many women as men were looking after elderly or handicapped relatives. For many, caring is additional to domestic and wage labour. Sixty per cent of women are now in full- or part-time employment. Finally, although no party supports institutionalized care as the ideal, the point was made that it should be available when necessary. Yet, in the early 1980s, many local authorities reported the closure of some residential homes and the reduction in staffing levels of those that remained.

Politics and social policy clearly affect the quality of care. However, the precise organization of publicly funded care is subject to professional as well as political opinion and, slowly but increasingly, also to the demands of the old themselves. Although some old people's homes are humanely and intelligently run, a growing body of opinion questions whether often large, rather impersonal institutions provide the best social environment for old people. Certainly there seems little case for the 'younger', more active old to be in them. From the mid-

1970s there has been a rapid expansion of sheltered housing, a promising alternative to old people's homes. Butler, Oldman, and Greve (1983) define a sheltered housing complex as one which has 'a resident warden, an alarm system fitted to each dwelling, and the occupancy and dwellings being restricted to elderly persons'. There are now 400,000 sheltered housing units in use. As Butler and his colleagues point out, sheltered housing combines independence with dependence, one's own house with ready access to care. Their own survey of 800 residents in twelve local authorities found that the quality of housing and the general physical environment of most respondents had 'most significantly improved by a move to sheltered housing'. Their main criticism is that too often the old are not involved in 'active partnership' in the sheltered community. Indeed they state that the theme of their book, *Sheltered Housing for the Elderly*, was that the consumer had been 'relatively' ignored. However, they do find some decline in 'stereotypical thinking' about the old on the part of those involved in the sheltered housing movement, and the tone of their work is cautiously positive.

Policy alternatives

Support for *universal* rather than *selective* benefits has been a traditional aspect of socialist thought on social policy in Britain. The National Health Service is the major monument to this approach. The state pension is another example of universalism. Socialists such as Peter Townsend argue that the old age pension ought to be raised to the point where it provides a decent standard of living. Nearly 20 per cent of pensioners get supplementary benefits in addition to their pensions and, according to Department of Health and Social Security estimates, a further 900,000 pensioners are eligible but do not claim (presumably, in many cases, because they regard it as demeaning to do so). Townsend's calculations are that two-thirds (five million) of the elderly live in or on the margins of poverty. The Conservative government rejects a substantial rise in the old age pension in real terms on the grounds that those in need can be provided for by the supplementary benefits system, and that a large global increase would increase public expenditure, taxes, and inflation. There is no doubt that the old have been caught up in the debate of the early 1980s about scarce resources. What has to be decided is whether their claim for a decent and dignified life should have priority over some other expenditures.

Finally, old people have cultural and educational as well as material needs. I find Philippe Ariès's description of the medieval school as open to those children and mature adults who needed it richly suggestive. The idea could be expanded to include the old. Many a class would be enlivened by rare experience and commitment to learning as a result. This might be a start to building a community to which the old belong just as much as the rest.

Activities

1 Compare the various institutions in which old people may end their lives.
2 Discuss whether the dependency of the elderly in Britain has been socially constructed.

Further reading

Carver and Liddiard An Ageing Population *(1978) is an excellent reader and I acknowledge its usefulness to me in writing this chapter. The one aspect it lacks is coverage of the recent growth of Marxist thought on old age. Phillipson (1982) fills this gap and is very readable. I am conscious of not having covered the autobiographical and biographical material available on old age in this chapter. Gladys Elder's* The Alienated: Growing Old Today *(1977) is both tough and moving. Ronald Blythe's* The View in Winter: Reflections on Old Age *(1979) contains authentic, unsentimental material on the rural old.*

References

Abrams, M. (1959) The Teenage Consumer. *London Press Exchange Papers* No. 5.

——(1964) *The Newspaper Reading Public of Tomorrow.* London: Odhams.

Abrams, P. (1972) Age and Generation. In P. Barker (ed.) *A Sociological Portrait.* Harmondsworth: Penguin.

——(ed.) (1978) *Work, Urbanism, and Inequality: UK Society Today.* London: Weidenfeld & Nicolson.

Adler, R. (1970) Radicalism and the Skipped Generation. *Atlantic Monthly* 225 (February): 53–7.

Anderson, M. (1980) *Approaches to the History of the Western Family 1500–1914.* London: Macmillan.

Ariès, P. (1962) *Centuries of Childhood.* London: Jonathan Cape.

Ball, C. (1981) *Beachside Comprehensive: A Case-study of Secondary Schooling.* Cambridge: Cambridge University Press.

Barker, P. (ed.) (1972) *A Sociological Portrait.* Harmondsworth: Penguin.

Barthes, R. (1972) *Mythologies.* London: Paladin.

Benedict, R. (1934) *Patterns of Culture.* Boston: Houghton Mifflin.

143

Berg, I. (1970) *Education and Jobs: The Great Training Robbery*. Boston: Praeger.

Berger, P. and Berger, B. (1976) *Sociology: A Biographical Approach*. Harmondsworth: Penguin.

Blythe, R. (1979) *The View in Winter: Reflections on Old Age*. London: Allen Lane.

Bottomore, T. (1967) *Critics of Society: Radical Thought in America*. London: George Allen & Unwin.

Bowles, S. and Gintis, H. (1976) *Schooling in Capitalist America*. London: Routledge & Kegan Paul.

Braverman, H. (1974) *Labour and Monopoly Capital*. New York: Monthly Review Press.

Butler, A., Oldman, C., and Greve, J. (1983) *Sheltered Housing for the Elderly*. London: George Allen & Unwin.

Carver, V. and Liddiard, P. (1978) *An Ageing Population*. London: Hodder & Stoughton in association with the Open University Press.

Cashmore, E. (1979) *Rastaman: the Rastafarian Movement in England*. London: Unwin University Books.

Cashmore, E. and Troyna, B. (1982) *Black Youth in Crisis*. London: George Allen & Unwin.

Clarke, J. (1976) Style. In S. Hall and T. Jefferson *Resistance through Rituals*. London: Hutchinson.

Claver, J. and Spitzer, J. (eds) (1970) *The Chicago Conspiracy Trial*. New York: Bobbs & Merril.

Cloward, R.A. and Ohlin, L.E. (1961) *Delinquency and Opportunity*. London: Routledge & Kegan Paul.

Cohen, A. (1955) *Delinquent Boys: The Culture of the Gang*. New York: Free Press.

Cohen, P. (1972) *Subcultural Conflict and Working-class Community*. Birmingham: CCCS.

——(1982) School for Dole. *New Socialist* October/November.

——(1984) Losing the Generation Game. *New Socialist* April/May.

Cohen, S. (1979) *Folk Devils and Moral Panics*. 3rd edn. London. MacGibbon & Kee.

Commission for Racial Equality (1981) *Race Relations in 1981: An Attitude Survey*. London: CRE.

Commission of the European Communities (1982) *The Young Europeans: An Explanatory Study of 15–24 Year-Olds in EEC Countries*.

Corrigan, P. (1979) *Schooling the Smash Street Kids*. London: Macmillan.

Cowgill, D.O. and Holmes, L. (1972) *Aging and Modernization*. New York: Appleton-Century-Crofts.

Crick, B. and Robson, W.A. (1970) *Protest and Discontent*. Harmondsworth: Penguin.

Crisp, Q. (1981) *How to Become a Virgin*. London: Fontana.

Dahrendorf, R. (1959) *Class and Class Conflict in Industrial Society*. London: Routledge & Kegan Paul.

de Mause, L. (1976) *The History of Childhood*. London: Souvenir Press.

Douglas, J.D. and Waksler, F.C. (1982) *The Sociology of Deviance: An Introduction*. Boston: Little Brown & Co.

Downes, D. (1966) *The Delinquent Solution*. London: Routledge & Kegan Paul.

Easterlin, R.A. (1980) *Birth and Fortune: The Impact of Numbers on Personal Welfare*. New York: Basic Books.

Eisenstadt, S.N. (1956) *From Generation to Generation*. London: Collier-Macmillan.

Elder, G. (1977) *The Alienated: Growing Old Today*. London: Writers' and Readers' Cooperative.

Erickson, E. (1963) *Childhood and Society* 2nd edn. New York: W.W. Norton.

Feuer, L. (1969) *The Conflict of Generations*. London: Heinemann.

Fiske, M. (1979) *Middle Age: The Prime of Life*. New York: Harper & Row.

Fletcher, R. (1966) *The Family and Marriage in Britain*. Harmondsworth: Penguin.

Freeman, D. (1983) *Margaret Mead and Samoa: The Making and Unmaking of an Anthropological Myth*. Harvard: Harvard University Press.

Fuller, M. (1982) Young, Female and Black. In E. Cashmore and B. Troyna (eds) *Black Youth in Crisis*. London: George Allen & Unwin.

Gaskell, G. and Smith, P. (1984) Are Young Blacks Really Alienated? *New Society* 14 May.

Gleeson, D. (1983) *Youth Training and the Search for Work*. London: Routledge & Kegan Paul.

Goldthorpe, J.H., Lockwood, D., Beckhofer, F., and Platt, J. (1969) *The Affluent Worker in the Class Structure*. Cambridge: Cambridge University Press.

145

Goldthorpe, J.H. *et al.* (1980) *Social Mobility and Class Structure.* Oxford: The Clarendon Press.

Gordon, M.M. (1978) *Human Nature, Class, and Ethnicity.* Oxford: Oxford University Press.

Gould, J. and Kolb, W.L. (eds) (1964) *A Dictionary of the Social Sciences.* London: Tavistock Publications.

Haber, C. (1983) *Beyond Sixty-Five: The Dilemma of Old Age in America's Past.* Cambridge: Cambridge University Press.

Hall, S. and Jefferson, T. (1976) *Resistance through Rituals: Youth Subculture in Postwar Britain.* London: Hutchinson.

Hall, S., Critcher, C., Jefferson, T., Clarke, J., and Roberts, B. (1978) *Policing the Crisis: Mugging, the State and Law and Order.* London: Macmillan.

Halsey, A.H., Heath, A.F., and Ridge, J. M. (1980) *Origins and Destinations.* Oxford: The Clarendon Press.

Hampden-Turner, C. (1971) *Radical Man: The Process of Psycho-social Development.* London: Anchor Books.

Handy, C. (1984) *The Future of Work.* Oxford: Basil Blackwell.

Hargreaves, D. (1967) *Social Relations in a Secondary School.* London: Routledge & Kegan Paul.

Harrington, M. (1962) *The Other America.* Harmondsworth: Penguin.

Harris, L. and Associates (1975) *The Myth and Reality of Aging in America.* Washington DC: National Council on the Aging.

Hebdige, D. (1979) *Subculture: The Meaning of Style.* London: Methuen.

Hendricks, J. and Hendricks, C.D. (1977) *Ageing in Mass Society.* London: Winthrop.

Hepworth, M. and Featherstone, M. (1982) *Surviving Middle Age.* Oxford: Blackwell.

Hilgard, S. R. (1979) *Introduction to Psychology.* London: Harcourt Brace.

Horne, J. (1983) Youth Employment Programmes, a Historical Account of the Development of 'Dole Colleges'. In D. Gleeson (ed.) *Youth Training and the Search for Work.* London: Routledge & Kegan Paul.

Ingham, R. (1978) *Football Hooliganism.* London: InterAction Imprint.

Jacobs, P. and Landau, S. (eds) (1967) *The New Radicals: A Report with Documents.* Harmondsworth: Penguin.

Jefferson, J. (1976) Cultural Responses of the Teds: The Defence of Space and Status. In S. Hall and T. Jefferson *Resistance through Rituals.* London: Hutchinson.

Lacey, C. (1970) *Hightown Grammar*. Manchester: Manchester University Press.

Lacy, W.B. and Hendricks, J.L. (1980) Developmental Models of Adult Life. *International Journal of Aging and Human Development* 11: 89–110.

Lasch, C. (1970) *The Agony of the American Left*. London: André Deutsch.

Laslett, P. and Wall, R. (1975) *Household and Family in Past Time*. Cambridge: Cambridge University Press.

Levitson, D. (1978) *The Seasons of Man's Life*. New York: Knopf.

Lipset, S.M. and Raab, E. (1971) *The Politics of Unreason*. Chicago: University of Chicago Press.

McRobbie, A. (1978a) Working-class Girls and the Culture of Femininity. In A. McRobbie *Women Take Issue*. London: Hutchinson.

——(1978b) *Women Take Issue*. London: Hutchinson.

McRobbie, A. and Garber, J. (1976) Girls and Subcultures. In S. Hall and T. Jefferson (eds) *Resistance through Rituals*. London: Hutchinson.

Maddock, K. (1973) *The Australian Aborigines*. Harmondsworth: Penguin.

Malinowski, B. (1957) *The Sexual Life of Savages*. London: Routledge & Kegan Paul.

Mannheim, K. (1952) *Essays on the Sociology of Knowledge*. London: Routledge & Kegan Paul.

Marcuse, H. (1964) *One Dimensional Man*. London: Routledge & Kegan Paul.

——(1969a) *Eros and Civilization*. London: Sphere.

——(1969b) *An Essay in Liberation*. London: Beacon Press.

Marsh, P. (1978) Life and Careers on the Soccer Terraces. In R. Ingham *Football Hooliganism*. London: InterAction Imprint.

Marsh, P., Rosser, E., and Harré, R. (1978) *The Rules of Disorder*. London: Routledge & Kegan Paul.

Mead, M. (1971) *Coming of Age in Samoa: A Study of Adolescence and Sex in Primitive Societies*. Harmondsworth: Penguin.

Merton, R. (1938) Social Structure and Anomie. *American Sociological Review* 3: 672–82.

Miller, W. (1958) Lower Class Culture as a Generating Milieu of Gang Delinquency. *Journal of Social Issues* 14: 5–19.

Musgrove, F. (1964) *Youth and the Social Order*. London: Routledge & Kegan Paul.

Naipaul, S. (1982) The Rise of the Rastaman. *The Observer* 27 June.

National Children's Bureau (1976) *Britain's Sixteen Year Olds*. London: NCB.

Neutgarten, B.L. (1974) Age in American Society and the Rise of the Young-Old. *Annals of the American Academy* September: 187–98.

Nisbet, R. (1970) Who Killed the Student Revolution? *Encounter* 24 (February): 10–18.

O'Donnell, M. (1981) *A New Introduction to Sociology*. London: Harrap.

——(1983) *New Introductory Reader in Sociology*. London: Harrap.

Osborn, A.F., Butler, N.R., and Morris, A.C. (1984) *The Social Life of Britain's Five Year Olds: A Report of the Child Health and Education Study*. London: Routledge & Kegan Paul.

Parker, S. (1971) *The Future of Work and Leisure*. London: George Allen & Unwin.

Phillipson, C. (1982) *Capitalism and the Construction of Old Age*. London: Macmillan.

Pilkington, A. (1984) *Race Relations in Britain*. Cambridge: University Tutorial Press.

Pryce, K. (1979) *Endless Pressure: A Study of West Indian Life Styles in Bristol*. Harmondsworth: Penguin.

Radcliffe-Brown, A.R. (1952) *Structure and Function in Primitive Society*. London: Oxford University Press.

Rampton Report (1981) *West Indian Children in Our Schools*. London: HMSO.

Reich, C. (1970) *The Greening of America*. London: Allen Lane.

Rex, J. (1982) West Indian and Asian Youth. In E. Cashmore and B. Troyna (eds) *Black Youth in Crisis*. London: George Allen & Unwin.

Rex, J. and Tomlinson, S. (1979) *Colonial Immigrants in a British City*. London: Routledge & Kegan Paul.

Roberts, K. (1984) *School Leavers and Their Prospects: Youth and the Labour Market in the 1980s*. Milton Keynes: Open University Press.

Robins, D. and Cohen, P. (1979) *Knuckle Sandwich: Growing Up in the Working-class City*. Harmondsworth: Penguin.

Rogers, D. (1972) *The Psychology of Adolescence*. New York: Appleton-Century-Crofts.

Roszak, T. (1973) *The Making of the Counterculture: Reflections on the Technocratic Society and Its Youthful Opposition*. London: Faber.

Rowntree, B.S. (1901) *Poverty: A Study of Town Life*. London: Macmillan.

St John-Brooks, C. (1984) Mother and Child Together. *New Society* 17

May: 262.

Scarman, Lord (1982) *The Scarman Report: The Brixton Disorders 10–12 April 1981*. Harmondsworth: Penguin.

Sheehy, G. (1981) *Pathfinders*. London: Bantam Books.

Shils, E. (1969) Plenitude and Scarcity. *Encounter* 23 (May): 37–57.

Smith, D.J. (1977) *Racial Disadvantage in Britain: The PEP Report*. Harmondsworth: Penguin.

Steinberg, I. (1982) *The New Lost Generation: The Problems of the Population Boom*. New York: St Martin's Press.

Teodori, M. (1970) *The New Left: A Documentary History*. London: Jonathan Cape.

Titmuss, R. (1959) *Essays on the Welfare State*. New Haven: Yale University Press.

Townsend, P. (1957) *The Family Life of Old People*. London: Routledge & Kegan Paul.

——(1979) *Poverty in the United Kingdom*. Harmondsworth: Penguin.

Trowler, P. and Riley, M. (1984) *Topics in Sociology*. Cambridge: University Tutorial Press.

Tylor, E.B. (1871) *Primitive Culture*. London: John Murray.

Venner, M. (1984) In D. Weir and E. Butterworth (eds) *The New Sociology of Modern Britain: A Reader*. London: Fontana.

Watts, A.G. (1983) *Education, Unemployment, and the Future of Work*. Milton Keynes: Open University Press.

Whyte, W.F. (1955) *Street Corner Society*. Chicago: University of Chicago Press.

Willis, P. (1977) *Learning to Labour: How Working-class Kids Get Working-class Jobs*. Farnborough: Saxon House.

——(1984a) Youth Unemployment: 1 A New Social State. *New Society* 29 March.

——(1984b) Youth Unemployment: 2 Ways of Living. *New Society* 5 April.

——(1984c) The Land of Juventus. *New Society* 12 April.

Willmott, P. (1966) *Adolescent Boys of East London*. London: Routledge & Kegan Paul.

Index

153

154